Portfolio Design for the Accessories Designer

Shenlei E. Winkler

Fashion Research Foundation Publishing
New York, NY

Other Books by Shenlei E. Winkler

Shengri La Spirit: The Making of OpenSim from a Designer's Point of View
Designing Dreams: The Art & Business of Avatar Apparel Design & Development

Portfolio Design
for the
Accessories Designer

Copyright © 2011
Fashion Research Foundation

All rights reserved. No part of this book covered by the copyright hereon may be reproduced or used in any form or by any means – graphic, electronic, or mechanical, including photocopying, recording, taping, or information storage and retrieval systems – without express written permission of the publisher.

Library of Congress Control Number 2011924975
ISBN-13 978-0-9841171-2-3
ISBN-10 0-9841171-2-1

All trademarks and registered trademarks are the property of their respective owners. Adobe®, Photoshop®, Illustrator®, DreamWeaver® and InDesign® are owned by the Adobe Corporation.

Dedication

Dedicated to the family and friends who believe and make it all possible.

Mom, Dad, Gila, Aimee, Calli, Chris,

Michele, Lillie, Barbara, Karen Ann, Linda

Thank you.

Acknowledgements

No book makes it into print without the assistance of other people. In the case of a book aimed at fashion designers, other design professionals and educators contributed to the growth and evolution of this book in various ways. From school assignments to work projects, their wisdom and guidance helped form our insight into what makes a design concept strong, and how to best present design ideas in the most saleable way.

A huge round of thanks go out to:

- My father, Ed Winkler, who gave me his set of rapidograph pens when I entered the scientific illustration phase of my program at the University of Michigan;

- My mother, Sue Winkler, who continues to explore her artistic abilities and who is a shining example of getting her work out there.

- Howard Crum, at the University of Michigan Herbarium, whose exacting requirements for the Moss Flora of Mexico project taught me to hand black line with an anal retentive degree of precision;

- Sandra Jo Adam, who edited out the whiches and thats and was extraordinarily good-tempered about it all.

- Vasilios Christofilakos, head of the accessories department at FIT whose expertise in sketching accessories was exceptionally helpful;

- And the numerous other people whose inspiration has proven so helpful and valuable.

Thank you to all.

Shenlei Winkler
March 2011
New York City, NY

Table of Contents

Preface   13

Introduction   15

Chapter 1: Presentation Is Key   24

    Choosing a Size   26

    Choosing an Orientation   29

    Choosing a Portfolio Cover   32

    Choosing Paper & Printing   46

    Inserts & Page Protectors   49

    Budgeting for Your Portfolio   52

    Managing Your Portfolio   60

Chapter 2: The Student Portfolio   67

    Defining the Student Portfolio   68

    When Student Portfolios Are Useful   69

    Why You Shouldn't Spend a Lot on Your Student Portfolio   71

Table of Contents

Moving Beyond the Student Portfolio	73
Chapter 3: The Professional's Portfolio	**81**
What Are the Critical Differences?	82
Adding a Resume	84
Portfolio Management	88
Chapter 4: Contents of a Portfolio	**103**
Table of Contents	106
Introducing…Yourself!	108
Telling Stories Visually	115
Designing Collections	123
Process & Technique	126
Media Coverage and Awards	135
Supporting Cast	137
Taking a Bow	139

Table of Contents

Chapter 5: Portfolio Etiquette   **143**

    Presenting to Educators   146

    Presenting to Your Peers   162

    Presenting to Recruiters   165

    Interview Etiquette   183

    Things To Remember - Best Practices   194

Chapter 6: Beyond the Book   **205**

    Resources & References   206

    Tools   219

Conclusion   **228**

Table of Contents

Gallery of Collections:

Carriage Trade	17
Canopy	33
Blue	54
Latte	75
Nautical Dreams	94
Optimism	109
Cyberealia	127
Royal	153
Werd!	169
Spring Romance	184
Ponytale	199
Fierce	209

Preface

My motivation for writing about this topic stemmed from a conversation I had with several of our summer interns at the Fashion Research Institute. As part of the exercises we had set for them, I was showing them my book (portfolio to the non-practitioner). As we flipped through the pages, and I answered their questions and showed them how portfolios are put together and presented, I realized that much of what I was sharing was not information I had gained from design school, but rather education gained from the school of hard knocks. This book is the result of both my experiences and that single pivotal conversation.

What *Portfolio Design for the Accessories Designer* is specifically designed to do is to show how portfolios get created by the individual accessories designer. Design students, applicants to design schools, and recent graduates will all find this book helpful. Using examples drawn from my own portfolio, I will show you what it takes to have a professional, well-developed portfolio, using the best practices that we teach through our classes at the Fashion Research Institute. Our practices have evolved specifically from my successes in job hunting and working in the industry. These 'insider secrets' are exactly the things you need to successfully develop and show your design portfolio to potential employers and design schools, and any place you need to be able to demonstrate your design skills to maximum effect.

There are other portfolio books available. I bought every one of them on the market that I could find when I was preparing my portfolio. None of them showed me what I needed to know about putting together a portfolio that really worked for me as an accessories designer. Nor did they offer me a hint at how much time I would have to devote to my portfolio, or how much I should expect a job-winning portfolio to cost to produce. This book addresses these specific considerations, as well as providing a clear visual guide to portfolio layout. Using examples drawn from my personal portfolio, you will learn how to develop visual stories that move the viewer through the portfolio and showcase your design talents and skills.

A good portfolio has the capacity to materially assist designers in every phase of their career to advance to the next level. It is my belief that all designers will benefit from these specific guidelines and best practices for the creation of a successful portfolio.

Introduction

Your portfolio is the single most important project you will create while in design school. We would argue that it is so important that design students should be provided with an orientation seminar at the very beginning of their design education that focuses on nothing but their portfolio. The reason we think this is because of the sheer volume of work and the final bottom line cost that will be required of the student to produce a portfolio that will enable them to obtain work in the apparel industry. Students will be engaging in a great deal of work in any event in order to complete all the requirements for their design degree. It would be better if they could guide their work more constructively to develop projects and concepts that ultimately support the development of a comprehensive portfolio with several well-defined visual stories.

Our suggestion to you is to flip through this book and look at the pictures several times before you decide to read the text. This is a heavily illustrated book, and the visual stories provided here were taken from the actual portfolio of a successful designer. Learning what makes a winning visual story will help you create your own successful visual stories, and in turn create your own job-winning portfolio. The stories presented here are those of another designer and should not be copied in whole or in part to your own portfolio. For one thing, if you present a portfolio with images taken from this book and they are recognized as such, you will not get the job.

For another thing, the techniques used and skills required to create these particular visual stories are the techniques and skills of another unique designer. Unless you have those skills and abilities, you will be in trouble if your design director at your new job asks you to repeat something they saw in 'your' book.

Use the visual stories and concepts as inspirations to create your own unique portfolio—you will do a better job of interviewing and you do not ever need to worry about being caught for copyright theft or lack of creativity.

Carriage Trade
Autumn 2016

Carriage Trade is the signature collection developed for a branded property owned by Black Dress Technology. The pieces included in the collection are designed to be manufactured through several digital processes to allow the consumer to create their own mass-customized design.

The collection itself may be viewed within an immersive 3D marketing platform that combines social media marketing in conjunction with a very sticky experiential that enables brand loyalty. This collection needed to carry the look and feel of the brand for an equestrian lifestyle, and therefore uses such imagery as horses, foxes, and riders throughout the collection of prints and fashion neckwear. Since this is a 'living collection', the exact product classes will increase over time.

Prints and products shown here may be purchased on-line. Please visit the Black Dress Technology web site at http://www.blackdresstechnology.com for more information.

Carriage Trade
Autumn 2016

Chrome PMS 387	**Arctic** PMS White	**Flaxen** PMS 7499
Teal PMS 7476	**Olive** PMS 7483	**Peridot** PMS 378
Golden PMS 1495	**Bay** PMS 7533	**Grullo** PMS 877
Chestnut PMS 167	**Appaloosa** PMS 419	**Dapple** PMS 418
Sorrel PMS 490		**Charcoal** PMS 426

CARRIAGE TRADE
AUTUMN 2016

Winners
Polo

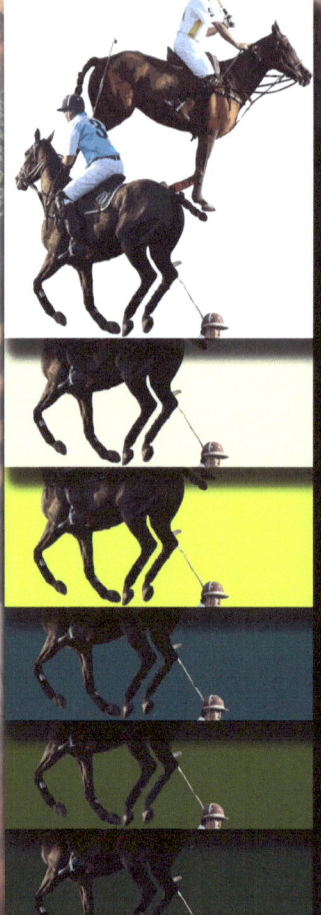

Arctic

Flaxen

Chrome

Teal

Peridot

Olive

Carriage Trade
Autumn 2016

Foxy   Tallyho!

- Arctic
- Flaxen
- Chrome
- Teal
- Peridot
- Olive

Carriage Trade
Autumn 2016

Big Red

Dressage

- Arctic
- Flaxen
- Chrome
- Teal
- Peridot
- Olive

Carriage Trade
Autumn 2016

Fashion Scarves

Arctic

Flaxen

Chrome

Teal

Peridot

Chapter One
Presentation Is Key

Chapter One
Presentation Is Key

In design, people do judge your book by its cover. Quite often how you have chosen to package and present yourself and your portfolio will have a direct impact on whether you are offered a position or not; and if you are, how substantial your compensation package might be. Therefore, the first thing we focus on is the physical presentation of your portfolio and the considerations you should take into account when developing your portfolio.

We will evaluate the following considerations: size, orientation, paper, printing requirements, inserts, the portfolio cover, your budget for your portfolio, and the management requirements you should consider for your portfolio. We'll also suggest some modern printing alternatives for your portfolio.

Choosing a Size

One of the first considerations you should take into account is the size of your final portfolio. Portfolios come in a range of sizes from tiny 6"x4" portfolios up to 18"x24" portfolios and larger. The most common sizes are 8.5"x11"; 11"x14", and 11"x17". The sizes reflect the size of the paper that is placed into page protectors inside the portfolio. The portfolio cover itself will be larger, making your final portfolio as much as two inches bigger around.

In selecting a size, consider the following points:

- Non-standard sized portfolios will present multiple challenges, including finding inserts and an appropriate printer to develop your product. While you will need to trim all of the pages you put into your book, non-standard sizes may present a real issue if you have to create and insert a last minute story to your book using your home printer.

- Larger sizes will cost disproportionately more than smaller sizes, because not only is the portfolio cover more expensive for the larger sizes, but also the page protectors, printing and even the paper is more expensive per sheet than for smaller sizes.

- Larger sized portfolios are heavier to carry around. This may not sound important, but try standing on your feet all day at a career fair while you are carrying a five-pound portfolio. This will quickly become obvious why bigger is not always better, and why editing your book into something manageable is preferable.

- Portfolios larger than 11"x17" are unwieldy and may not fit well on a design director's desk. You run the risk of accidents to your portfolio if you require a design director to look at a portfolio that won't fit easily on her desk. While you may (or may not) care what happens to the design director's desk, you will most certainly care if she accidentally knocks over a cup of coffee onto your expensive book while trying to open it.

- Portfolios larger than 8.5"x11" are difficult to manage at career fairs, where your reviewer is often standing and needs to manage your portfolio and flip through it by hand. Larger portfolios will present an issue for your reviewer, including simply finding enough space to open your book.

- Larger sized portfolios may present a challenge to have new pages printed for your book. Most design schools have graphics centers whose entire function is to print high quality images for faculty and students, and they will customarily provide an array of high quality printing options relatively inexpensively. This option usually vanishes when a student graduates, and for those who need nonstandard or oversized printouts the retail cost becomes astronomical.

- Finally, whatever size you choose, keep in mind you need to be able to change out your visual stories on a fairly regular basis. Home computers rarely offer more than an 8.5"x14" printing capability. Even then, that is not a full 8.5"x14" spread because home printers usually cannot print up to the edge of the sheet.

A final consideration you should take into account is that, generally, whatever size portfolio you start with will be the portfolio size that you carry with you into your professional life. Once you begin working, it is highly unlikely you will have the time or the interest to overhaul your portfolio in its entirety. You will of course keep it fresh and add in new pages from time to time, but completely overhauling your portfolio simply won't be an option, no matter how fast or skilled you are at creating pages for your book.

Choosing an Orientation

Portrait or landscape? That is the single burning question you should ask yourself. Individuals who are looking at your portfolio do not want to have to rotate your portfolio to view the pages. Pick an orientation and stay with it religiously. A completed portfolio is heavy – once you add up the weight of the papers, the ink, the inserts, and the actual case, your portfolio will easily weigh two pounds or more. It doesn't sound like much, but forcing your viewer to flip your portfolio around so they can view your pages in the proper orientation will quickly become tedious for him or her simply due to the weight. Most viewers are handling multiple books sequentially, and if yours is inconvenient to handle, it will stand out, but not in a good way.

Choose an orientation and stick with it. Portrait (meaning your portfolio is taller than it is wide) is more common than landscape (where your portfolio is shorter than it is wide). Landscape portfolios are usually put into the same cases as a portrait portfolio, but the spine runs across the desk parallel to the viewer. This means that the pages on the 'top' of the portfolio are further away from viewer and therefore harder to read. You probably lose 50% of the impact of the top pages in a landscape-oriented portfolio.

Portfolio Design for the Accessories Designer

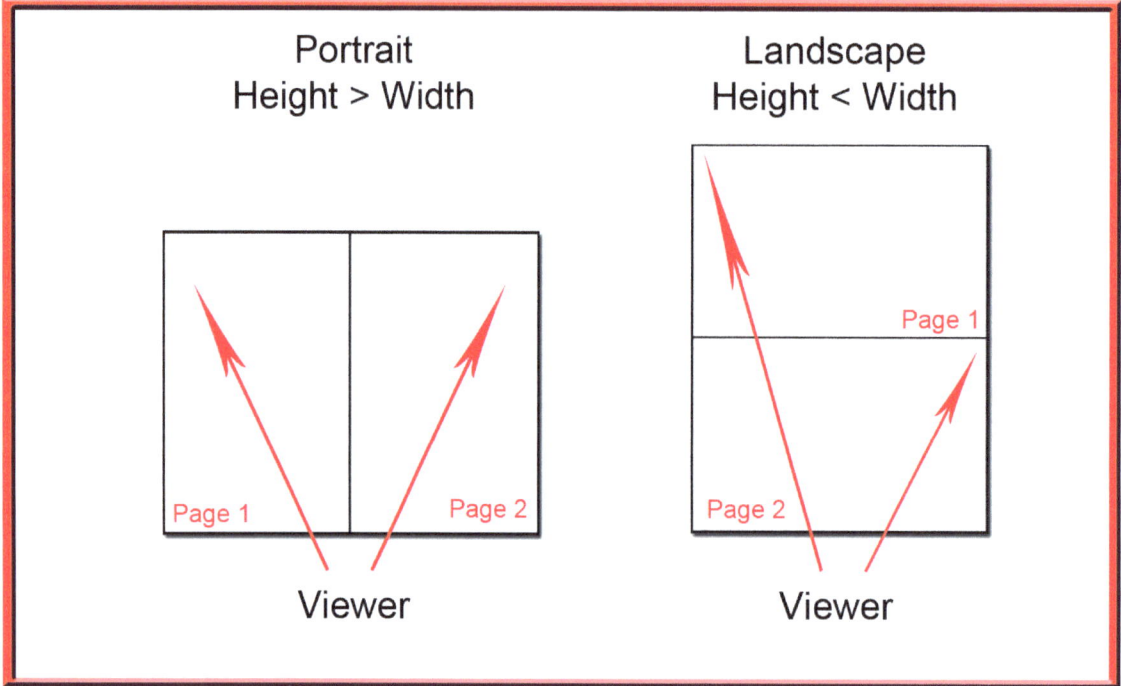

Portrait-oriented portfolios allow the viewer to see both pages at equal distance. In the West, the right hand page receives more initial scrutiny, but at least both pages can be viewed with the same level of acuity.

Portfolios that have a portrait orientation also have a huge advantage over landscape-oriented portfolios. It's easier to place your product on a portrait-oriented page than on a landscape-oriented page.

And lastly, with the increase in Print on Demand publishers, you can easily turn your portfolio into a perfect bound book that you can use for marketing purposes (often less expensively than having a complete portfolio created). Turning your 'book' into a book is lighter weight and you can worry less about having your portfolio stolen, since the original stays safely at home.

If you mix the orientation of the pages in your portfolio, make sure that the viewer never has to rotate your portfolio more than once. This means you start with portrait and finish with landscape, or start with landscape and finish with portrait, but you don't make the viewer have to rotate your book more than once. It's better to never make them rotate it at all, especially if you have chosen an oversized portfolio. If you think about how people's desks are laid out, common sense will tell you that from a purely self-interested point of view, you do not want your portfolio to be exposed to risk of the viewer knocking over a drink or a vase of flowers and possibly getting wet and ruined.

Best practices are to pick an orientation and stay with it.

Choosing a Portfolio Cover

Remember, your viewer will be judging your book by its cover, so you want to select a portfolio case or cover with this in mind. Your cover is the very first thing a hiring authority, a design director, or even your portfolio or sketch teacher will see. And while your teachers will be forgiving if you use a student portfolio to present your work in class, design directors and people who have the ability to hire you won't be.

Your cover should reflect the contents of your book, and it should reflect your design aesthetic. If you are a proponent of 'slow design' or traditional or classic design aesthetic, you may want a traditional leather cover, possibly with your name stamped in gilt on the spine. Students who prefer developing 'green' products may do well with a bamboo case. Those with a futuristic preference can do well with an aluminum or acrylic case.

Canopy is a collection of men's headwear developed for a mass market retailer. While this collection was not sold to the retailer, the development of the collection is similar to collections I sold to the same retailer in previous years.

Canopy incorporates colors and styles which are seasonally appropriate for the gender class. Note the absence of bright colors – while higher end lines may incorporate brighter colors, for this retailer, these are the sorts of colors that move well off their end caps and displays. The styles are classic styles as well: ivies, buckets, baseball caps, western hats, and broader-brimmed ranger hats.

The collection uses a variety of trims, which largely use less expensive production techniques such as a thermo-application and digital dying.

Moving through the collection, the viewer can see how the mood board incorporates the sense of masculine out-of-doors, with the colors of the mood board reflected in the color story. Iconography from the mood boards also appears in the trims developed for the collection (stag, ferns, and so on). This collection was developed using Black Dress Technology's design & development tool, Black Dress Design Studio, and shows the headwear developed in 3D models. The collection showcases the designer's ability to work with 3D modeling, a skill which is becoming increasingly important.

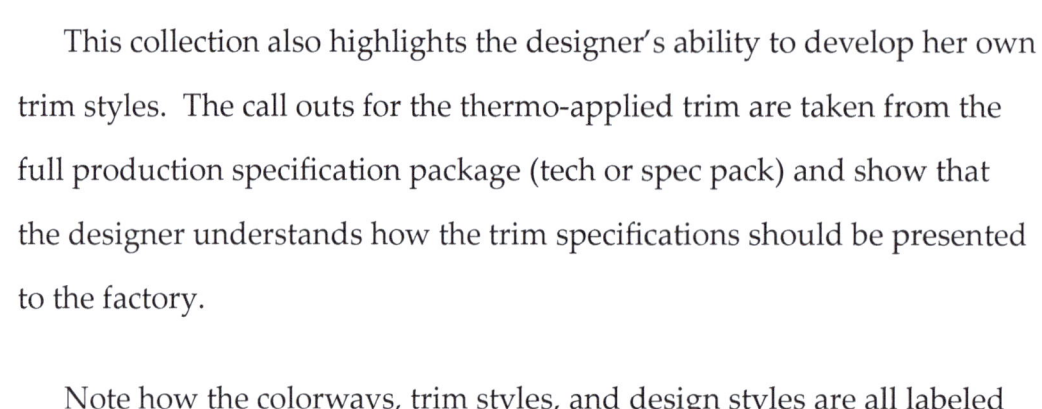

This collection also highlights the designer's ability to develop her own trim styles. The call outs for the thermo-applied trim are taken from the full production specification package (tech or spec pack) and show that the designer understands how the trim specifications should be presented to the factory.

Note how the colorways, trim styles, and design styles are all labeled with their name or style numbers. The colors are also labeled with an design house name and the color match number. This entire collection of documents, plus the actual tech packs for the trim and design styles can be sent to the factory to help reduce errors.

CANOPY

Spring 2010

CANOPY

Pine Needle PMS 16-6216	**Stone** PMS 18-1112	**Khaki** PMS 13-1006	**Vista** PMS 18-4011
Spruce PMS 19-0315	**Granite** PMS 19-1015	**Putty** PMS 16-1108	**Mountain** PMS 18-0201

Soot — PMS Black

Sorrel PMS 470-C
Quartz PMS 445-C
Goldrush PMS 4515-c

Arctic White PMS White

SPRING 2010

CANOPY

C/W 1

C/W 2

C/W 3

C/W 4

Spring 2010

CANOPY

Fern Print
C/W 1   C/W 2   C/W 3   C/W 4

Stag Print   **Cones Print**   **Full Moon Patch**

SPRING 2010

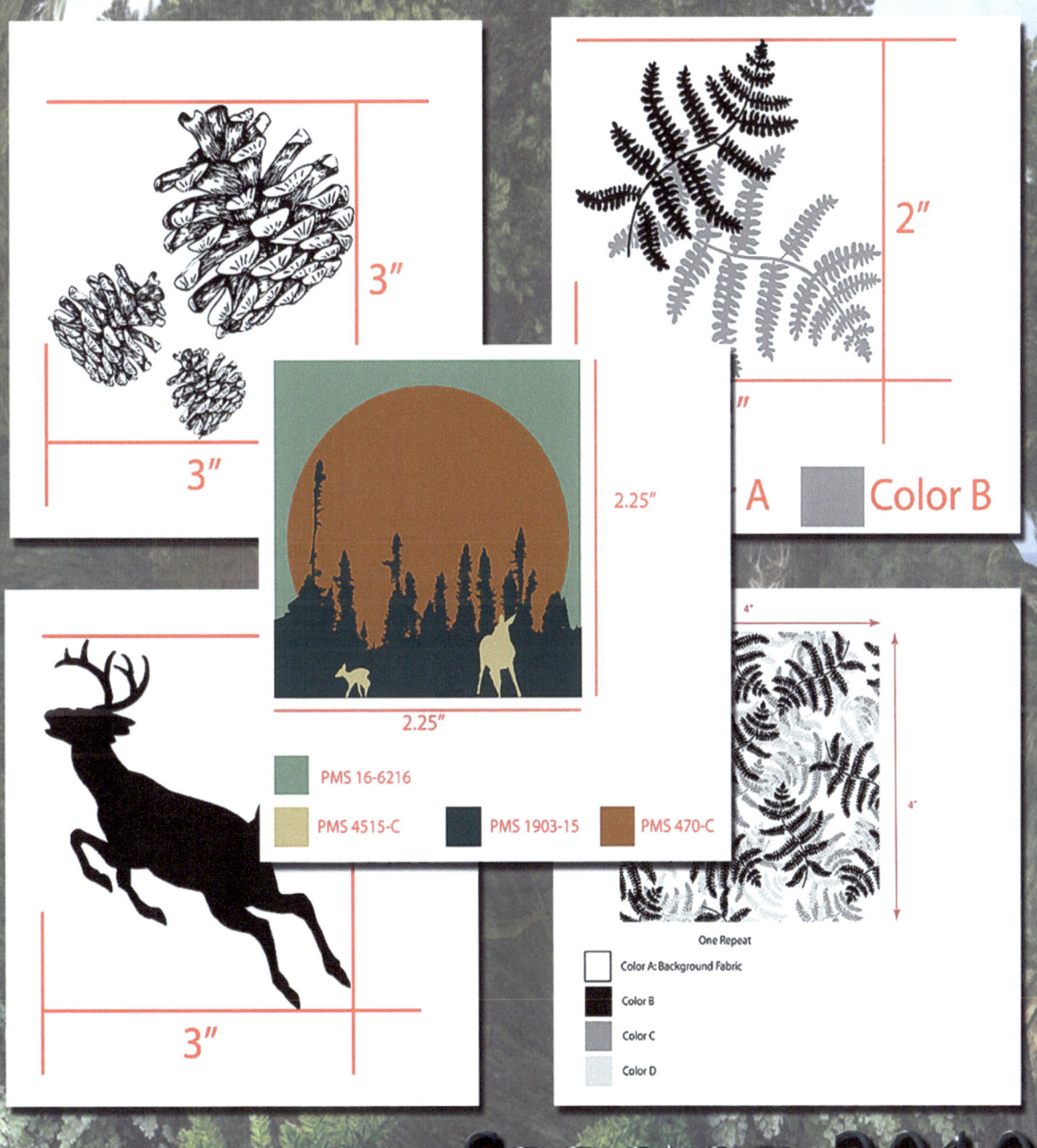

Canopy

1088

1089

1090

Spring 2010

In selecting your perfect cover, think about the following characteristics:

- Will the cover itself hold up well to being handled? Some covers, such as aluminum or acrylic, may be prone to scratching or denting, which will reduce their initial visual appeal. Some are fragile, especially in cold weather, and may fracture or break if dropped. Others may chip along the edges. Your cover needs to be perfect and to stay perfect, so think about a cover material that will literally weather anything you may throw at it.

- Is the cover material heavy? This is not something most students consider in selecting their portfolio cover, but as mentioned previously, having to stand around on uncarpeted floors at career fairs holding a heavy portfolio is not a great experience. You may not care, or think you don't care, but anyone who has had the experience of carrying a heavy portfolio around will quickly wish they hadn't chosen quite such a heavy portfolio cover!

- Does the cover reflect you, and your design aesthetic? The cover is the first thing your viewer sees, and you can often determine how well an interview or portfolio review will go depending on how they handle your book. Are they delighted with the first sight of your case, or do they have a look of disdain at your choice of case?

- How much do you have to spend on your case? This literally means that you have to think carefully about how much you are willing to invest in your case. Keep in mind that in purchasing your portfolio cover, cheaper is definitely not better. Your portfolio cover may not be replaced during your working career, and as you get more experienced, your additions will reflect your current work although not, perhaps, your interests. You want a portfolio cover that will be able to transition your career from student to experienced designer and to reflect your growing abilities and accomplishments.

- How durable is the cover's hardware? A portfolio consists of multiple parts; the outside is the obvious thing most designers look at, but the inner hardware is actually quite important. Most portfolios come as part of a system, which includes not just the cover, but also the inserts (page protectors) and the hardware used to secure the inserts and bind them into the cover.

Look at as many different systems as you need to in order to select a cover and system that works for you. Some systems will have relatively inexpensive covers, but the inserts and additional hardware will end up making the entire portfolio more expensive in the long run. A system that takes too long or requires special tools to change out pages may ultimately make you a little crazy, especially when you want to change your stories in your portfolio in between interviews and you can't do it easily.

The systems are often proprietary, which means they force you to buy their special cover/hardware/insert system and their products cannot be used in an alternative system. Plastic hardware may break more quickly than a metal hardware system; metal of course is heavier than plastic or acrylic.

Avoid a portfolio cover that uses a ring binder system. A 3-ring binder is not an acceptable portfolio system. The plastic page covers move around too much in such a system, which causes them to get scratched and bruised, which in turn makes them milky and hard to see through. Ring binders are cheap, but ultimately they will cost you time, energy and money to maintain your inserts that cover your pages. Ring binders are easy to add pages to, but because they don't hold your pages securely, ultimately the small additional effort you have to make to insert pages into a peg or screw system will be amply repaid because your inserts will remain clear and bright longer.

Only you can decide which cover to purchase, and you will want to start shopping for your cover well in advance of your need for it. Start shopping for your cover at least one semester or quarter before you graduate (if not more) so that you can look at as many choices as possible. Don't be afraid to try out any of the many web options - you can find almost anything you need on the web, often for less than at the student bookstore. There are a good many web sites that focus solely on portfolios, so do a web search and see what you turn up.

Choosing Paper & Printing

Everything that goes into your portfolio needs to receive as much consideration as you can possibly give it. This includes your choice of paper and the kind of printing you use to produce your pages. As a student, you will likely create your pages by hand or with your own color printer. Your courses will often require that you develop your sketches using hand techniques, and do mechanical layouts, using double-stick tape, specialty papers, and actual materials and your hand-drawn and colored sketches. In instances when you are requested to develop mood boards, themes, inspiration pages and additional work, your teachers will still likely accept them printed on your home printer using whatever paper you happened to have in the printer at the time.

Obviously, this haphazard approach will not work for your professional portfolio. Home printers produce un-calibrated images where the colors are often color-shifted in one direction or another. They cannot print to the edge of the sheet, so you have a narrow white border around all sides of your page. In general, even high-quality photo papers don't accept and display the ink as well as commercial equipment. There is an order of magnitude in the difference between a commercial printer and a home printer, including the substantial difference in the actual sizes that can be produced by the commercial printer.

In choosing papers for your book, you want heavy weight papers that accept color well. Your school graphics facility will usually have a paper portfolio you can look at, so you can feel the weight of the paper. Most of the time you will want a smooth paper with a satin or gloss finish, but occasionally you may want to produce your portfolio on a paper that has a finish such as a laid or woven pattern.

This is particularly nice for portfolios where you are developing a portfolio reflecting your ability to design ecologically sound or 'green' garments, accessories and footwear. Whatever paper you choose, you must use it throughout your portfolio, so choose carefully. Most students will opt for one of the easily located smooth calendar-rolled papers with either a satin or a gloss finish.

In selecting a finish, keep in mind that gloss finishes, while visually arresting, may be difficult to interchange in plastic page covers because the gloss tends to catch on the inside of the page protectors. Matte finishes are dull and may cause your color to appear muddy and dim. Satin finishes are less brilliant than the gloss finishes, and can be more easily added or removed from the plastic page protectors. Gloss finishes may also be a bit more expensive, but we have always felt that a gloss finish with its brilliant colors was worth the extra expense and the additional time required for insertion into page covers.

Different printing machines give a different quality of print work. Ask to see samples from the different machines. We've had very good luck having our pages printed on a commercial Xerox® printer, but Canon® also makes an exceptional color printer. Your local print shop expert will be able to best guide you if you tell them what you're doing. They may have good suggestions about how to set up your files for printing, and they can make your life so much easier if you simply ask for their advice and help in advance.

Whatever paper and finish you choose, plan to use them throughout your portfolio. Changing a paper and/or finish midway through will make your portfolio look amateurish, with one exception. If you develop hand-collaged pages, you will obviously use a very different paper or papers to do this. These pages will be different from any printed pages you may include, but the printed pages should all use the same quality and weight of paper, and the print quality should be the same. In general, best practices require you to have your portfolio printed by the same printing facility, using the same papers and finish. This will ensure that your book is produced with the same quality throughout your portfolio from beginning to end.

Inserts & Page Protectors

Page protectors, sometimes called sheet protectors, are a critical component in your portfolio. These are transparent pockets that contain your pages and protect them from being scratched or damaged. Some page protectors fold over themselves and are open at the top and bottom. These usually have black paper inserts.

Page protectors, as with all other components in your portfolio, range in price and come in an array of quality. The least expensive page protectors are usually made of vinyl and are slightly dull and prone to bruising and scratching. While soft and flexible, vinyl page protectors are often less clear and bright than page protectors made of acrylic, Mylar®, polypropylene, or even some classes of polyester. Mylar page protectors are expensive, but have bright, sparkling qualities that enhance your printed pages. Mylar pages scratch easily, however, and may need to be replaced more often than acrylic or vinyl pages. Acrylic pages are a good first choice for the new professional who can't quite afford the maintenance for Mylar page protectors, but who want a brighter and more transparent page protector than the other materials provide. As of this writing, acrylic tends to crack and shatter more easily as it ages, and it can scratch more readily than the polyester page protectors.

In choosing a good page protector, make it a point to visit your local art or office supply store and look at the quality of the protectors. Only you can decide which material is the best for you, and you are the only who can decide which brand of page protector you prefer. Some portfolio systems have proprietary page protectors that only work with their particular binding system.

In such cases, you will usually have a choice between a lower end and a more expensive page protector. The lower end page protector is fine for your student portfolio, but you will need to invest in the higher end page protectors for your professional book. Look for page protectors marked archival quality and nonstick to ensure that your carefully printed pages are not damaged when you need to remove them from the protector.

Most of the time, you won't want to use inserts, which are thin, archival quality black paper that are placed between the leaves of the sheet protector. Inserts are common in student portfolios, which usually have lower quality page protectors. The insert helps assure that the leaves of the page protector do not stick together, and it provides substance to the page protector.

Make sure that your binding system has posts or rings that are spaced correctly for your page protectors. Some common manufacturers of page protectors include C-line and Avery-Dennison®. In general, plan to buy a box of 25-50 page protectors. A ten-page pack will be quickly consumed and these smaller packs are very expensive per page protector relative to the economy sizes. You will in fact use up that many page protectors in developing your visual stories.

Budgeting for Your Portfolio

Something that everyone seems to gloss over is planning for the expense of his or her professional portfolio. Very few design schools will come right out and tell students how much they should budget for this, probably because the bottom line figure is pretty overwhelming, and of course the amount of effort individual students will put into their portfolio varies so widely. Nevertheless, it is important to begin early to budget for your portfolio, because you will not only have to create projects that you will use in your book, but you will also have additional costs for the cover, inserts, printing and finishing.

By the time I finished printing our professional portfolio that I still use, I had spent over $3,500 USD. This figure included material costs for projects; costs for consumables (papers, markers, pencils, and so on); printing costs; and my portfolio system including the cover and inserts. This did not include the time I invested in developing my projects; laying-out and designing my pages; reordering my stories; and consulting with my local printer about the best printing options for my book. Nor did it include the time spent in actually designing how my finished book would look. I easily invested more than 800 hours in developing my final professional portfolio, which has yielded successful results in obtaining work in the apparel industry.

While these numbers may seem astronomical to you as a student, I would invite you to consider that 800 hours, spread out over 12 months, works out to be about 15 hours a week spent developing the single most important thing you should take from your experiences in design school.

And if this seems like too much work, please consider that a well-done portfolio will mean the difference between starting as an intern or assistant designer and starting as a more highly paid and valued design associate or full designer. Students who are serious about working in the apparel industry will budget and plan accordingly so that their final project, their portfolio, is the best quality they can afford in both time and money.

So, how much will it cost you? For starters, everyone has to buy a cover and insert system. Plan to spend between $85-500 for a professional quality portfolio cover. The lower end will include materials such as acrylic and bamboo while the higher end will include hand-made leather covers. Inserts will range in price, but in general plan to pay between $15-35 for a 25-50 page package.

Prices range widely for inserts depending on the material, the quality, and the number of pages. Economy boxes are less expensive per page, and you will certainly use as many pages as you have available. If you

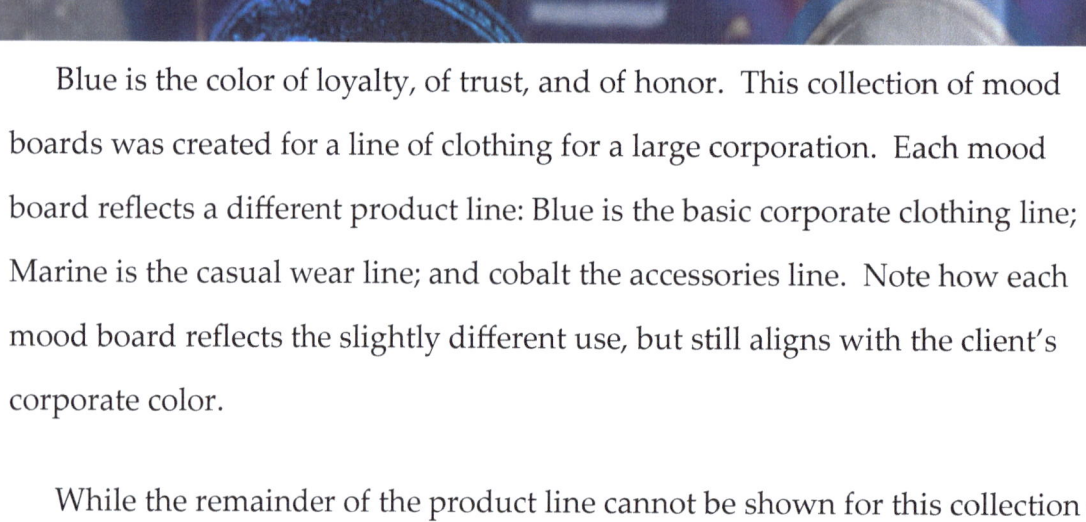

Blue is the color of loyalty, of trust, and of honor. This collection of mood boards was created for a line of clothing for a large corporation. Each mood board reflects a different product line: Blue is the basic corporate clothing line; Marine is the casual wear line; and cobalt the accessories line. Note how each mood board reflects the slightly different use, but still aligns with the client's corporate color.

While the remainder of the product line cannot be shown for this collection of products, the mood boards are nice examples of how to develop evocative boards to really help you carry the mood of your collection.

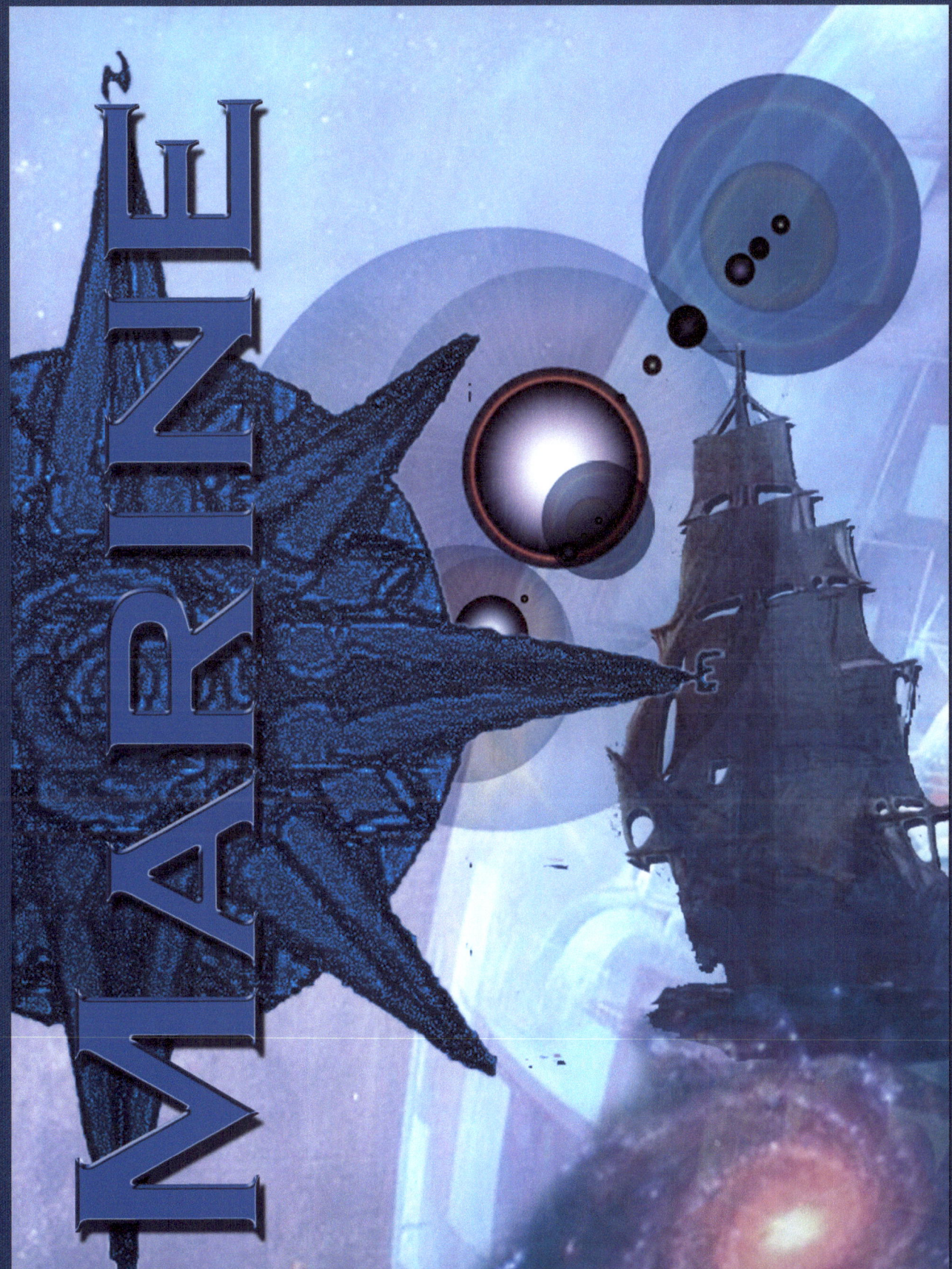

are concerned about the cost you can always split a box with a classmate if you both use the same size and system in your portfolio. You will need a minimum of 20 pages to start, but may well use up to 40. Additional post extensions and a portfolio case may also add to the bottom line - a portfolio case is well worth the $10-25 and we recommend buying one that is loose enough to allow your portfolio to slide in and out easily, but not so loose the portfolio moves freely about in it.

Post extensions will be required if you have many collaged pages or if you have a very great many visual stories, but most students starting out won't need them right away. Get them anyway, so that you have them when you do need them. There is nothing worse than needing that extra 1/8" or 1/4" of clearance in your portfolio and not having it.

Your projects will have their own materials costs, which will be determined by the types of projects you design and create. In general, start thinking of your work and projects in the terms of a collection. Your early work will be discarded, even if you include it in your student portfolio, because it simply will not be as high quality as the work you create later in your career. Nevertheless, plan for these costs—your projects may well end up in your book, and you will want to make your items of the highest quality materials you can, so they photograph well.

Your art work will also carry costs you will need to budget for. In general, plan to spend between $300-450 on sketching materials, markers, pencils, erasers, papers, drawing guides, and pens. Use quality materials so that you can create quality images, some of which may well end up in your portfolio in one form or another.

In addition to your projects, you'll need some digital assistants: a high quality 10+ megapixel camera (between $125-$400), Photoshop®, a good quality scanner (scanners are inexpensive, you can get one that works well for under $150), a nice quality printer ($50-$150), and of course, a computer. Computers that are good enough to run Photoshop may cost as little as $500 (for a low-end PC) and up from there. You may also want to invest in a couple of large flash or thumb drives ($25-$100 each) and a pen tablet ($100-$2,500).

Direct production costs may include professional quality photography (which can run from $100-$300 an image) and of course, printing. Printing will cost $1-$54 a page, depending on your paper, the kind of ink, and the quality of the work.

Oddly enough, printing may be the least expensive part of this enterprise— assuming you make few mistakes. Low-end print jobs may be good enough to use for your portfolio; the higher end prints are usually specialty papers used mostly by graphic designers and artists. The point where printing becomes expensive is where you discover that you have made errors you need to fix and have to have your pages reprinted.

Here's an example budget for your portfolio. Keep in mind that your actual budget will vary depending on what you choose to spend for the various components. This is one area you cannot try to hunt for bargains, however. A good book will get you into the game with a good job and a good salary. Plan ahead both for the expense and for the amount of time you will need to create the projects to develop your visual stories.

Sample Portfolio Budget
(based on costs in 2005)

Project Item	Cost
Portfolio Cover	$95
Page Protectors	35
Portfolio Case	15
Printing (100 pages)	200
Photography	350
Project Costs	2,250
Camera	100
Art Supplies	425
Resumes	30
Total	$3,500

Managing Your Portfolio

This is an important part of your whole portfolio. Creating filing systems that make sense to you, so you can quickly find your work again, will be critical to you when the time comes to put your professional portfolio together.

You might think, as you are starting out, that you don't have enough material to worry about managing your portfolio, and so you dump papers, sketches and other things you create into a giant stack somewhere or you are casual about setting up your files in your computer. Begin as you plan to go on—set up a filing system.

It doesn't have to be fancy, and it doesn't need to follow along with anyone else's filing system. As long as you can quickly find the files or the papers you need, and neither your files nor your physical objects (papers, projects, etc.) are in danger of being lost, damaged or discarded, then your system can be said to work just fine for you.

There are some things all system will have in common, however, and these are the best practices that you need to incorporate into your own portfolio management.

You will have three types of things you need to manage: project assets, digital assets, and hardcopy or paper assets. Project assets include all of your materials, art supplies, and finished projects (but not hard copy, or paper).

Digital assets include such things as images, Excel® and Word® files, and Photoshop® and Illustrator® files. Your digital assets may also include movies, podcasts, and your blog or web site with the related files used not to create them. Hardcopy assets include your sketches, prints, photographic prints, and all other print outs or sketched images.

Project assets may seem to be the easiest to manage because they are (usually) physically large enough to require at least a little attention to not lose parts or to avoid damaging them. Nevertheless, if you follow a few best practices, you will find managing your project assets will be made much easier.

First, invest in a couple of large plastic dump bins, such as the kinds that are used to store blankets or other linens. Also invest in 3-4 smaller sized plastic bins. You will also need several large manila envelopes. Obtain some plain white tissue paper (archival is best, but if you can't afford it, at least get plain white flat fold tissue). Also, purchase some hang tags - plain oaktag with reinforced holes and plain string hangers are fine. Lastly, if you haven't already purchased some fine-tipped black Sharpies® for your pattern making now's the time to stock up.

Store your materials and equipment in the plastic bins. Label each project using the hangtags: it's easy to forget when something was made, or what patterns were used to make it, so make sure you include all the details such as the date of construction, the class you made it for, what patterns were used, and with what collection the project was made.

You may also want to include the names of any related digital files that reference this project. Make sure you wrap tissue around your finished projects and clearly mark the dump bins with each project included in each one. Unused materials should be rolled or folded, wrapped in tissue and stored in bins.

Never fold leather—it will crease and will be almost impossible to remove the crease marks left by folds. Take particular care to place layers of tissue between the grain and the skin side of any hides before rolling them up together. Take swatches of all materials you place in dump bins, pierce a hole in them, and string them together on a hang tag. This way you will know precisely what is in your dump bin(s).

You should also add a couple of packets of silica gel (save the ones that come in shoe boxes to use for this purpose) to any leather projects. While most leather is chrome tanned and remarkably stable, damp leather can mold and mildew over time. Woolen fabrics should be stored with your preferred method of moth control, to avoid damage to the fabric from moth caterpillars.

Use the manila envelopes to store your patterns. Make sure your pattern pieces are properly labeled before placing them in an envelope. If you have a sketch or image of the finished project, paste it to the envelope front, then label the envelope with the name of the project, the class you made it for, and so on.

Do not ever make the mistake of mixing all of your pattern pieces together—at some point you will want one of your patterns, and not being able to pull the correct one(s) will be both time consuming and a source of great frustration, especially if you know if you have the exact pattern but can't find it.

Hard copy assets should be filed appropriately, and stored in a large file bin. Make sure you file all parts of a given project together, from sketches to completed pages. Take care to lay your work into the file folder carefully so the edges do not get bent or wrinkled. If you have worked in a nonstandard medium, such as charcoal or pastel, you may need to use a fixative on it, and add special overlays of tissue or acetate to prevent the images from being smeared. Hard copy assets need to be kept away from light and heat so that they do not fade or yellow.

Create a filing system that allows you to easily locate your old sketches and other work. Use a grouping system that makes sense to you — whether grouping by project, type of style, or class, make sure you can easily locate any particular sketch, tear sheet, or other hard copy asset. Remember, it is your system so you are the one for whom it has to make sense.

Finally, your digital assets are something that requires the greatest amount of care, and which are very easy to be casual about. It is very easy to forget to back up your files, and very easy to lose them if your computer fails. Make sure you have three backup copies at all time - your files on your usual computer; files on a backup external hard drive; and files on back up CDs.

Get in the habit of backing up your files on a regular basis, because it can be almost assured that at some point you will forget, and it is at that precise moment that your hard drive will fail. It's quite amazing how regularly hardware fails at critical moments, such as when you absolutely have to get a new story developed and printed.

Develop a system that allows you to find your files easily. Use subfolders to sort out your work according the story you are creating or the project you are working on, and use sub folders to sort out the types of files you will create for each story.

Regardless of whether or not you begin in hardcopy, your portfolio will ultimately end up being largely a collection of digital assets, and it is critically important that you not only set up your filing system following a standard convention that you create, but also to make sure you follow it religiously.

It may seem to you unnecessary or excessive to worry so much about your digital files, but you will need them, or at least some part of them, all throughout your working life. Make it easier on yourself and be careful in setting up your filing system, and in filing your work in its respective folders.

Store all of your finished portfolio pages and your portfolio in the same place. Put your portfolio system parts, page protectors, inserts if you use them, and old stories together so that you can readily find them. Make it your habit to scan and photograph each new project as you complete it and file the imagery in the correct subfolder of your portfolio directory. Practice doing this as you go along so that when the time comes for your final assembly, you do not have to rush around and try to set up lighting and or scanners. Best practices call for staying organized both in your physical filing system and in how you work with your projects that will ultimately end up in your portfolio.

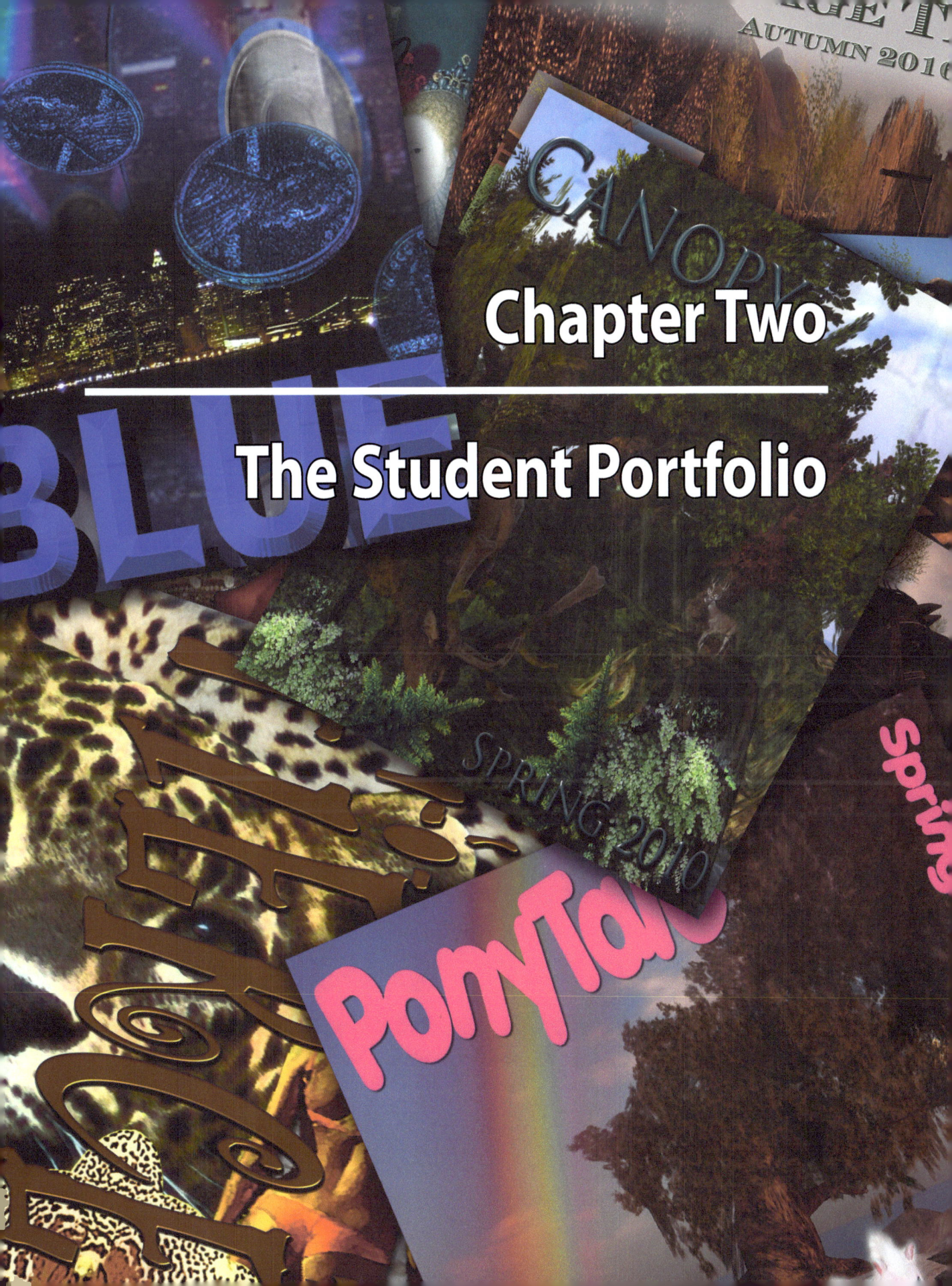

Chapter Two
The Student Portfolio

Defining the Student Portfolio

The student portfolio is simply an inexpensive case that you use to showcase your work for your current classes. These cases are often entire, meaning you cannot change the number of pages in the case. They are usually made of a heavy flexible polypropylene or polyester cover, and come in the same range of sizes as the portfolio covers. The page protectors included with the student system are usually heavier and quite often prone to bruising, scratching and smearing.

Unlike portfolio covers, the student portfolio is fairly inexpensive ($15-35). Student portfolios should not be considered as a possible substitute for the professional portfolio. These starter portfolios are intended as lightweight workhorses that you can use to transport your work, organize it, and keep it from being damaged, but should not be mistaken as an acceptable portfolio system for the professional portfolio that you are trying to develop.

The student portfolio looks exactly like what it is - an inexpensive practice book. Do not ever make the mistake of using one of these in any sort of presentation beyond design school. The quality of the portfolio system itself will reduce your credibility as a designer if you use the student portfolio to present to anyone who may wish to hire you.

You do need, however, a student portfolio, while you are in design school. Intoya® makes a good basic portfolio that will keep your pages from moving around too much in the cover. An inexpensive 1/2" 3-ring binder can also be used for your student work, although it is not ideal for a variety of reasons, including the fact that the ring spacing usually is not correct for most page protectors, and these binders only come in sizes designed for 8.5"x11" pages.

When Student Portfolios Are Useful

Student portfolios are necessary to properly present your work to your professors while you are in school, and later as a storage device for selected pages. Student portfolios are sturdy workhorses—they are designed to take quite a lot of abuse and they are reinforced accordingly.

Because student portfolios have been set up to display your work, you may find using them invaluable to keep a record of your homework and projects for your classes, which will serve as the basis of your later reference library. Design school is intended to prepare you to work in the industry, and you may find that you have questions as you are working that you have answers for from your classes.

Keeping your work organized in a student portfolio allows you to readily locate the answer from old homework assignments and class notes.

You may also find student portfolios useful to organize your tear sheets or references, or for use in creating a print library of swatches. Use archival glue sticks to paste swatches onto board and label each swatch. Since they are visually distinctive, it is easy to locate them in a bookcase or filing cabinet.

Why You Should Not Spend a Lot On Your Student Portfolio

The student portfolio is critically important in design school, but it should not be used outside of design school. Your professors have been through design school themselves, and understand the costs and demands of your education. They will not expect you to have a professional portfolio system that you will use to show your work to them.

Moreover, given the nature of design school, you will not want to expose your professional portfolio to the possibility of damage or worse, theft.

Your student portfolio should be sturdy and as cheap as possible. Depending on the classes you are taking, it may be exposed to an array of potentially damaging substances and experiences.

Accidents happen, and they happen more frequently as a semester goes on and your classmates (and you) get tired. Liquids get knocked over, things get dropped, and your portfolio could be in the way of any of these things and end up stained, torn, or worse.

Anything you put into your student portfolio should be replaceable.

Portfolios get stolen in design school on a regular basis, particularly if you set your tote or backpack down for a moment in a library 'just to go get a book in the stacks.'

It is regrettable that you have to be so vigilant about your work, but, if you are not, at some point you may find some light-fingered person has carried off your portfolio. This could be devastating if you do not have copies of your work—either scans or prints. While it is also virtually impossible to watch your belongings at all times, you should get in the habit of being aware of your portfolio and its location.

Your portfolio is more than just the physical case; it also contains your lifeblood as a designer—your work and your designs. You are a designer; so coming up with new designs should be as simple as breathing for you. However, you do not want your ideas stolen wholesale, so be aware of your book, and who has access to it.

Moving Beyond The Student Portfolio

The student portfolio (cheap, sturdy, lightweight) is a mandatory companion during design school, but it is not suitable for your use when you are ready to interview. Your instructors may tell you when the time comes to go purchase a professional portfolio, but if they don't then you should plan to purchase it in the last year or last semester of your education.

If you are seeking a four-year degree, you will have a fairly good idea of who you are as a 'brand' by the time you start your last year. You should begin looking seriously at portfolio systems so that you can purchase one in your next to last semester. Students matriculated in one- and two-year degrees may not know who they are as a brand till their last semester.

In either case, don't leave the portfolio search till the end. Start early, shop a lot, and look at a lot of covers and systems. Design students who are attending schools away from the major metropolitan areas will be hampered by their lack of access to stores with a wide range of systems, so these students need to plan ahead so they can mail order, and if need be, have time to return systems that are not appropriate.

Make sure you budget for the professional portfolio. It makes a huge difference in how you are perceived in interviews and career events.

Please do not think you can get by with a student portfolio. Anyone working in the field knows exactly what they are looking at when they see a cheap student portfolio used to present work - lack of respect for your own work, and lack of respect for the process of obtaining work. If you think it is somehow appropriate to present your work in a professional context using a system designed for student work, think again.

This is a visual industry, and you will be judged as much by your ability to present your work properly, and your understanding of how your work should be presented, as by your actual skill, talent, and creativity. Using a student portfolio where you should have a professional portfolio shows you do not understand your industry.

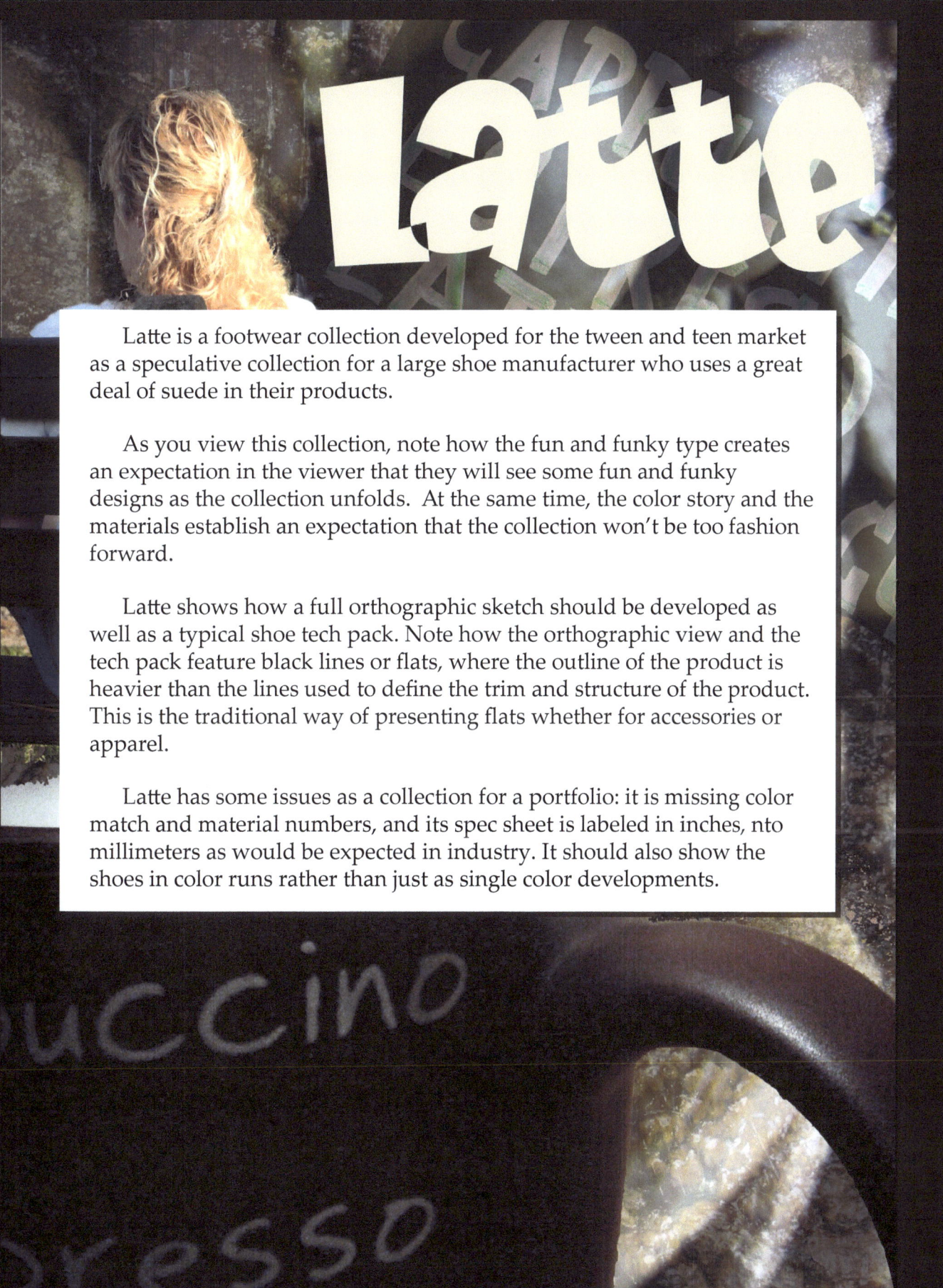

Latte

Latte is a footwear collection developed for the tween and teen market as a speculative collection for a large shoe manufacturer who uses a great deal of suede in their products.

As you view this collection, note how the fun and funky type creates an expectation in the viewer that they will see some fun and funky designs as the collection unfolds. At the same time, the color story and the materials establish an expectation that the collection won't be too fashion forward.

Latte shows how a full orthographic sketch should be developed as well as a typical shoe tech pack. Note how the orthographic view and the tech pack feature black lines or flats, where the outline of the product is heavier than the lines used to define the trim and structure of the product. This is the traditional way of presenting flats whether for accessories or apparel.

Latte has some issues as a collection for a portfolio: it is missing color match and material numbers, and its spec sheet is labeled in inches, nto millimeters as would be expected in industry. It should also show the shoes in color runs rather than just as single color developments.

Latte

uccino

resso

Latte

Materials

Au Lait

Espresso

Coffee

Robusta

Cappuccino

Mocahino

Suede **Calf** **Hardware**

Merchandise Group:	
Season:	Spring 2007
Factory:	Ki-Woon #3
Interim #:	SP07-04
Gender:	Female
Last:	Latte #2
Construction	Cemented & Vacuformed
Pattern Name:	Ooh-La-Latte
Date:	2-Apr-06

Wholesale Cost	$ 28.57
Retail Cost	$ 49.99

Stitching:	6 sti, #69 nylon to match	Heel:	Crepe Rubber Chunky High Heel
Binding:	Cappuchino Suede	Heel Height:	3.25"
Lining:	Cappuchino Suede	Footbed:	Dense cell PVC marshmallow foam
Sock Lining:	Mochacinno Calf	Midsole:	Crepe rubber & steel shank
Sock ID Logo:	Woven, 1.5"	Sole Edge Finish:	n/a
Outsole:	Crepe Rubber	Welt/Trim:	n/a
Outsole Logo ID:	Poured/colored crepe rubber, see	Outsole Materials:	Crepe Rubber
Hardware:	#2 antiqued brass grommets, 6	Packing Specs:	boxed, #2 box
Laces:	#12 nylon with nylon aiglette	Production Sizes:	5-10.5 in half sizes, B width
Additional Logo(s):	#4 Hang tag		

Notes: Poured crepe rubber sole with poured outsole logo (see attached diagram); stitching to match. Shoe made in following colorways: Au Lait/Espresso; Coffee, Robusto, Espresso; Cappuccino, Mochachino, Espresso.

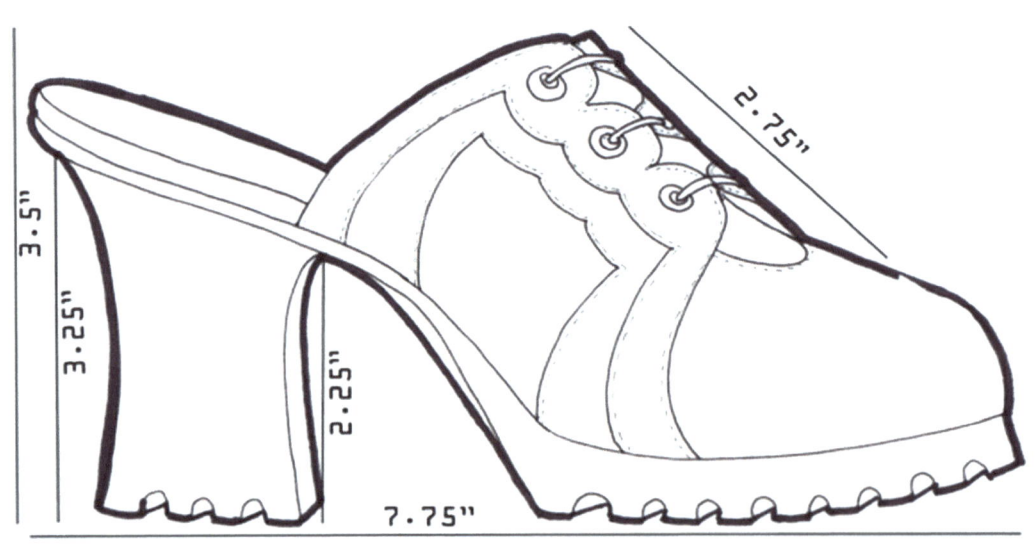

Portfolio Design for the Accessories Designer

Chapter Three
The Professional's Portfolio

What Are The Critical Differences?

We discussed the student portfolio in the last chapter and made references to the differences between the student portfolio and the professional portfolio. We did not, however, delve into the critical differences between the two, although by now you are likely getting the sense it may have something to do with cost.

Clearly, your professional portfolio is expensive—expensive to purchase the base materials, expensive to create, and expensive to maintain. Everything about the professional portfolio is more expensive than the student portfolio, and it should look like it.

Even more than the expense of the professional portfolio, however, is the obvious polish of the professional portfolio. Everything that goes into your professional portfolio has been reviewed, critiqued, reworked, and scrubbed until it is the best work you can possibly create. You have put a great deal of thought into the ordering of your professional portfolio, determining which layout best tells the story of your design ability.

Student portfolios largely follow a chronological order, where the early work shows less polish than your later work. This is very different from your professional portfolio, where everything that is included in the portfolio needs to be developed to your best ability and highest standards of workmanship.

Your professional portfolio is the ultimate form of self-marketing. Not only are you using it to showcase your specific technical skills of sketching, Illustrator® and Photoshop® work, and technical and line design, you are also using it to showcase your talent and design ability.

Lastly, you are showing potential employers that you understand how the marketplace works, and that you can speak both the language of design and business. You do this through the types of pages you create to enhance your visual stories, the ordering of your stories, and the kinds of stories you include.

Adding A Resume

While it is true that creative workers have a bit of leeway in creating their resumes, it is also true that your resume will be seen by more than just the design director or designer with whom you hope to work. Your resume will have to pass a series of gatekeepers who range from the human resources department to receptionists at employment agencies.

These gatekeepers are less likely to appreciate nonstandard resumes for the simple reason that they are looking for specific keywords and information on your resume. If this information is not included, your resume will be 'filed should they have an opening that requires your specific talent'—in other words, never looked at again.

Should you positively insist on having a creative resume, then you will need two versions - one for your portfolio, and one that will pass the screening process.

The resume you develop to pass the screening process should include your specific design and development skills such as sketching, pattern making, fitting, and of course, all of your computer skills. Keep your resume simple and to the point—you want a job in the apparel industry and everything you include on it should be directed to this goal.

For most design students just starting out, using a functional resume layout is better than a chronological layout. This of course assumes that you have the sorts of skills that the apparel industry needs. In cases where you have previous industry experience, a chronological layout may be preferable.

Each job seeker is an individual and his or her backgrounds are ultimately what will determine which layout is best for them. The key differences between the chronological and the functional resume is that the chronological resume focuses on the specific jobs held whereas the functional resume forces the focus to the actual skills and abilities of the job-seeker with actual job experience being included after the job skills and educational entries.

Regardless of the layout you choose, make sure you include the major programs that apparel industry companies are seeking: Illustrator, Photoshop, Excel, as well as any specialty programs you may have taken classes for such as ColorMatter®, or any of the database, pattern making or product development management software. Also add any professional certifications you may have completed and any awards or media coverage you may have gotten.

Never add anything to your resume that isn't accurate or true. This is a tactical, practical industry and if you have never even seen an Illustrator art board then listing Illustrator as one of your areas of expertise is a great way to go down in flames in an interview.

You should never include the following on your resume: your references or any suggestion of when you'd be available to start work. With regards to your references, you want to be able to warn them in advance that they may be receiving a call, and you want to get some sort of head's up from the potential employer that they are interested enough in you to go further.

With regards to your availability, anything you say about that will smack of desperation, and you really have no way of knowing how long someone has had your resume...or how old it is.

For example, we had someone call us about a resume of ours that they had found on some job site. The position they wanted us for sounded a little low level for where we were currently in our career and it wasn't till we discussed salary that we realized they had an old version which didn't reflect either our current skill set or our current salary. They had picked up the resume from a job aggregation site that had picked it up who knows where...three years before.

It would have been even more embarrassing for both parties if we had indicated we were immediately available for work on the resume, since at the time they called, we weren't looking.

Save all your awards and other bits and pieces and store them in a file folder. You will need this information when you sit down to create the first draft of your resume, and you do not want to have to scramble around trying to find the one last missing piece of information.

See if you can have a trusted instructor help you by reviewing your resume, or make an appointment to speak with a career counselor at your school. Start early with this—you will need your resume for more things than job hunting, and it's a difficult document to create.

If you are actively interviewing, make sure you include contact information including a current e-mail address and a cell phone number where you can be reached.

Finally, get an e-mail address with a respectable service, and don't try to be humorous in creating your email address. Humor is one of those not-so-funny things that can go badly awry. The last thing you want to do is offend a reader with the authority to hire you.

There are plenty of good resume books on the marketplace that will help you create a successful resume. New job seekers in particular should invest in two or three of these books and plan to rework their resume several times.

Your polished resume should be saved to a Word file for email purposes and job boards, as well as printed out on high quality cotton rag paper. Add a special pocket at the back of your portfolio and keep 10-15 copies of your resume in it. You may need more if you are attending a career fair or any of the many apparel trade shows.

Portfolio Management

Managing your professional portfolio takes more effort than managing your student portfolio. Your student portfolio is a chronological, linear development of your coursework, and it is designed to show your instructors how your skills are developing or where you need help.

The professional portfolio should be fully polished and the skills and talent displayed throughout the book should be homogenous throughout, with the same high level of ability shown at the beginning, middle and end.

You will reorder your professional portfolio on a regular basis, both as you add new stories and remove older, less polished stories, and as you need to order your book in order to change the focus for a particular audience.

Unlike the student portfolio, where you want to show your work in chronological order, the professional portfolio is subject to frequent change. The order of your stories will be determined by the emphasis you wish to place on given skills or talents you have relative to the position or competition for which you are showing your book.

It is important that you keep all of your pages protected at all times, whether they are currently included in your portfolio or not. It is a good idea to get a cheap version of your portfolio system (a less expensive cover that uses the same insertion hardware) to store any pages not inserted in your professional portfolio.

Pages that are not placed in a page protector are subject to damage not just from the possibility of being wrinkled or torn, but also from the possibility of the print fading due to sun damage or the printed side being bruised or scratched. Keep pages from the same story together in the storage binder.

You will also want to know which stories you have that you can pull from. Create a short table of contents or a list telling you what stories you have available. You may want to write a short description about the story you have created—it does not need to be more than two-three sentences, just enough to let you know what your concept was when you created the story, and what it was created to demonstrate.

Unlike the student portfolio, which is largely chronological and where the flow of the stories follows your course syllabus, the professional portfolio requires you to think about how you will order your pages to tell the story of your ability or skills.

This is where things become confusing for most students. How do you know what goes first, and what sort of stories will you create? What does it mean to create a story? Where do you start?

We have been discussing visual stories as though you know what a visual story is, or how it is developed. If you have never heard the term before, a brief definition of a visual story is the equivalent to a short story in English class. Like a short story, a visual story has an opening and a closing; it has a cast of characters; it has a plot; it has forward direction; and it has stylistic motifs, all of which come together to create, one hopes, a coherent message.

Visual stories differ from the English class short story by virtue of the fact that visual stories are told in images and motifs rather than in words. The visual story's cast of characters includes styles instead of characters; the plot is the overall layout and creation of the collection, and its motifs are iconography and symbols.

As you will see in the next chapter, the visual story is as difficult a proposition to create well as the short story is, and requires as much care and focus developing a compelling, interesting tale to the viewer.

We said that the visual story is not unlike a short story of words. But the portfolio itself should be thought of as a necklace of beads, with a single point of entry, or clasp. Each bead, or visual story, needs to be perfect in its own way, but all of the beads strung together need to create a harmonious whole. A necklace that is too short won't work; a necklace that is too long may not work either.

Ultimately, you must decide what sort of portfolio will work best for you, but we can offer guidelines that will help you keep your necklace of visual story beads from being too short, or too long. In any event, when you are developing your portfolio, keep in mind that every bead, every visual story, must be as close to perfect as you can make it.

Do not make the mistake of adding in a visual story that is inferior simply to make your portfolio longer. It will stand out (and not in a good way), and your viewer may be confused about what you hope to accomplish.

By now it should be clear that your professional portfolio will be an expensive document and a time-consuming project to create. It is safe to

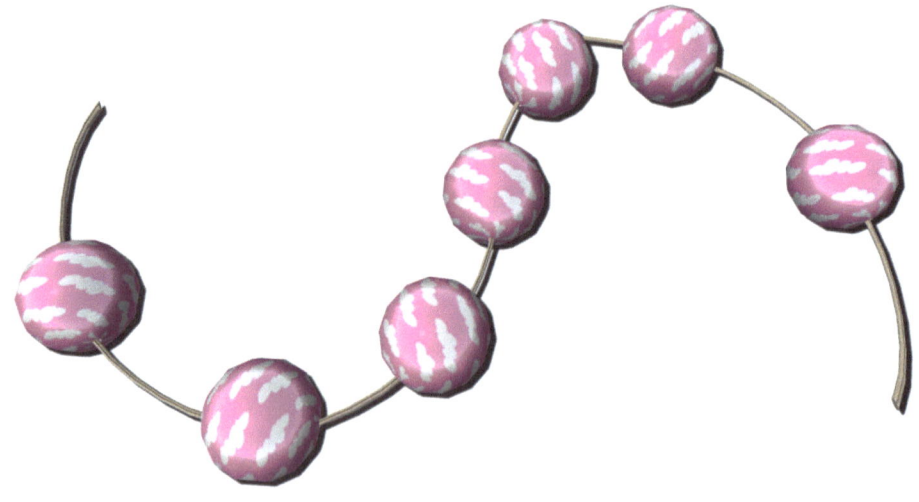

say that your book will probably be the single most expensive project you ever create.

It is equally safe to say that this is the one project in design school you must do your absolute best in creating and developing, because it is the marketing piece upon which your future in the highly competitive apparel industry will be determined.

By now you are no doubt biting your nails in frustration, because it is difficult to create something if you have never been exposed to the process. The next chapter covers specifically how to go about creating the portfolio that will help further your career in the apparel industry.

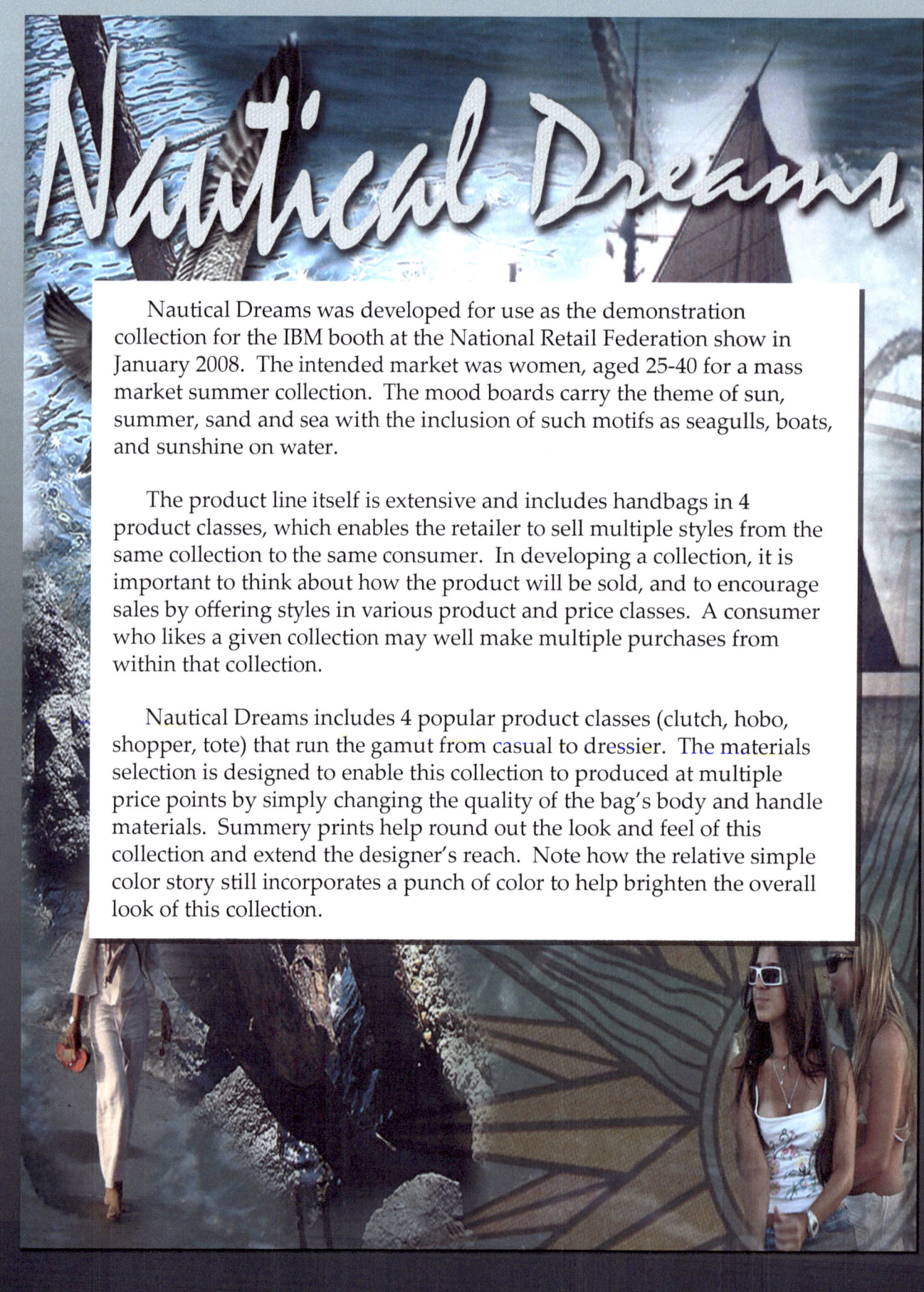

Nautical Dreams

Nautical Dreams was developed for use as the demonstration collection for the IBM booth at the National Retail Federation show in January 2008. The intended market was women, aged 25-40 for a mass market summer collection. The mood boards carry the theme of sun, summer, sand and sea with the inclusion of such motifs as seagulls, boats, and sunshine on water.

The product line itself is extensive and includes handbags in 4 product classes, which enables the retailer to sell multiple styles from the same collection to the same consumer. In developing a collection, it is important to think about how the product will be sold, and to encourage sales by offering styles in various product and price classes. A consumer who likes a given collection may well make multiple purchases from within that collection.

Nautical Dreams includes 4 popular product classes (clutch, hobo, shopper, tote) that run the gamut from casual to dressier. The materials selection is designed to enable this collection to produced at multiple price points by simply changing the quality of the bag's body and handle materials. Summery prints help round out the look and feel of this collection and extend the designer's reach. Note how the relative simple color story still incorporates a punch of color to help brighten the overall look of this collection.

Nautical Dreams

Clutches

Nautilus   Conch   Cowrie

Nautical Dreams

Shoppers

Breaker **Horizon** **Sand Bar** **Beach**

Chapter Four

Contents of a Portfolio

Chapter Four
Contents of a Portfolio

In this chapter, we get into the heart of the portfolio. Your finished, streamlined, professional portfolio may include up to fifty pages. More than that and your viewer will lose focus and interest. Ideally, you want your professional portfolio to contain 35-40 pages, and include four to six visual stories.

You may have fewer stories if your stories themselves include many pages, but you should never go beyond seven fully developed stories. Most viewers actually lose their ability to remember how many stories they saw in your book after they view seven stories, and if you have four pages a story, you are already up to thirty pages in your portfolio.

By the time you add your cover title page, and your conclusion page, you don't have many pages left to showcase any of the other things you will want to include such as any media coverage you've gotten or any awards you have received.

The precise number of pages you incorporate into your portfolio will vary depending on your use of it. When you attend career fairs and other cattle call events, you will want a stripped-down, lean portfolio with perhaps two-four solid stories. Shorter is definitely better with regards to events with long lines and a lot of competition.

The people who will be viewing your portfolio will already be short on patience and sleep, and stressed out from having to meet so many new people, review their resumes, and sometimes their portfolios. They simply will not have the attention span to look at your portfolio in any great depth.

Don't make it harder for them to remember you. Offer them a short and stellar version of your portfolio to scan through, and let them know you have a more comprehensive book to show at an actual interview. If they like what they see, not only will they be eager to see more, but also they will be thankful that you understand the challenges of their work at a career fair. They will remember you—positively!

Even if this is not enough to convince you, take it from us that standing in long lines holding onto your book, which will become increasingly heavy the longer you're there, only to have your book looked briefly or worse, not reviewed at all, will quickly bring you to agreement.

Portfolios are as individual as the people who create them, and not all portfolios will include all of the sections we list here. Nor will all sections be appropriate to be included in a given portfolio, even if the designer has developed all of these sections. A portfolio is a living document that a designer changes in response to his or her need at the time, using the sections, visual stories, and additional pages you have created.

In all cases, though, the portfolio exists to showcase the designer and the designer's abilities. Always keep this goal in mind when you are creating new inclusions for your portfolio: if the inclusion does not serve your best interests by showing your best ability, do not include it.

Table of Contents

Most designers will not need a table of contents, because their book is a sequence of visual stories that blend and move from one tale to the next seamlessly. For most designers, a table of contents is merely one more thing that will need to be updated often - in fact, every time you add or change a visual story. Some designers include a table of contents if they have many contrasting skills they wish to showcase and want their viewers to be able to find them quickly.

Where a table of contents will be useful to all designers is if they chose to publish their book as a book, as mentioned earlier. All published books need to include a table of contents, and in this case you won't be moving your visual stories around so you will definitely want to create a table of contents to help your viewer navigate your published book.

Table of contents all follow the same format—they have a chapter title, perhaps a chapter subtitle, and of course, the page number where the chapter starts.

Your chapter title will be the name of your visual story (more on this in the next section). Your chapter subtitle may be a brief explanation of what your viewer is supposed to draw from the visual story. Hopefully they won't need this sort of direction, but if you have something you specifically want to them to learn from your visual story, definitely add a chapter subtitle.

Although your portfolio should be composed mostly of images and visuals, if you choose to publish your portfolio in one of the more permanent formats you may also want to add a very short description prior to the start of the visual story.

We used this technique in our collections shown here, but you will want to make your description even shorter. In our case, we have something we want you to learn from the stories included.

In your case, you will have something you want to convey, but not at the expense of the actual images. If you use a description, please take care to make it no more than two-three paragraphs, or less than 350-400 words. You are not selling words. You are selling your talent, skills, and design ability, and that is what your audience is (hopefully) buying.

Introducing...Yourself!

You have selected a compelling portfolio case to capture your viewer's interest. Now it is time to set the stage for the most important part of your portfolio, namely your own introduction. Your first page should always have your full name tastefully and artistically displayed. This is your 'title page' where you have a chance to tease the viewer about what they will see inside.

You can use any number of possibilities as a background for your title page: a collage of technique sketches, a special concept page, or you can even opt for a stark and simply elegant black and white version of your

Optimism is a commercial project of prints for headwear and handbags, again developed using Black Dress Technology's Black Dress Design Studio product. Scanning the collection, the mood board establishes a sense of optimism with the bright bars of oranges breaking through the darker grey striated background.

And this is what you see in the collection: a series of prints using oranges and greys in a variety of ways, all using squares and rectangles. This is one of the tighter collections, where the mood board is almost literally translated into the collection of prints. The collection of nine prints is each developed in three colorways, and the prints can be mixed and matched within a product to create a solid collection of products.

The collection was designed to be very commercial. The prints make up well as accessories and could be used for a fun and funky home furnishings line as well.

These prints were used in several prototype samples, and are currently available for purchase as yardage. Please visit www.shenlei.com for details. They will ultimately be used to enable mass-customization for consumers to purchase their own products made using these prints.

Optimism

A/W 2010

Optimism A/W 2010

Sunset PMS 171 C	**Tangerine** PMS 1585 C	**Kumquat** PMS 715 C
Pigeon PMS Black 7 C	**Sepia** PMS 411 C	**Bone** PMS 9184 C
Charcoal PMS PMS 419 C	**Ash** PMS Cool Gray 11C	**Dove** PMS 434 C

Optimism

A/W 2010

Chandelier

Mosaic

Stripes

Microdots

Triplets

name in powerful typography. You may want to add your URL if you have a web site or a digital portfolio, or if you use social media you may wish to add your LinkedIn® or Twitter® information.

A word of advice for designers using social media: be very careful not to mix your personal and professional lives. This is critically important since you never know who is looking at your profile, and the last thing that you want to happen is to have posted some foul-mouthed diatribe that your interviewer can access.

Also, negative things tend to stick around far longer than you might expect, so in general, if you think it is a bad idea to post something on your Facebook® or LinkedIn profile, you should err on the side of caution and not do it. (If you wouldn't want to see it on a billboard, don't post it!)

Your title page should tease the viewer and set expectations about what they are about to see. When you are presenting, this page will receive the least amount of scrutiny but is often critical to creating a sense of expectation in your viewer. Do not think that because your portfolio reviewer may flip past the title page quickly that you can afford to give this page any less than your best effort.

Telling Stories Visually

Your visual stories need to tell your viewer about your skills, your talents, your design sensibility, creative abilities, and your ability to understand and deliver what the marketplace is seeking. Each individual story will have a distinctive look and feel, and should align with trends currently in the marketplace.

Specific product and age/gender classes all have unique ways of presentation. If you are developing your portfolio with the idea of specializing in a particular area, you should definitely consult any of the in-depth portfolio books that are out there to get a better idea of the 'best' way to present your ideas.

In general, however, you should plan to develop a unique and interesting concept or mood board, a color story, and a material and trim story as well as three-four groupings of product.

Technical fashion designers or designers focused on trim or hardware development will want to focus more heavily on things like technical specifications, flats, and trim and embroidery specifications and samples. As a new designer starting out, it is not likely that you will be able to incorporate actual trimmings or embroideries, unless you pay to have your designs executed by a sample maker.

We like to open our visual story with a strong, compelling concept or mood board. The mood board sets the stage, or establishes the mood of overall collection. Mood boards are something we spend a lot of time on with our interns—we think it's important to get the mood board really right.

Mood boards should incorporate motifs you plan to use throughout a collection; draw from the colors in your color story; and reflect both the market you plan to sell to and the target audience of the collection. The mood board can be used throughout the collection as the backdrop for all of the other component parts that go into the visual story, including the materials, trims, color story, and looks or styles.

As you look through the stories we have included here, you will note that we use the mood board in a ghosted or pale version to provide a visual pathway through the story. You can also create a frame using complementing imagery to provide a common link throughout your visual story.

The ghosted mood board, set to perhaps 30-40% opacity, frames each of the next components, including your color story, which should appear next; your materials selections; your trims; and finally, your looks. Your color story should always be presented with each color given a specific name and a color matching system number.

The Pantone Color Match System® is the most commonly used color system, although there are other color systems that specific retailers may use. You can easily locate the precise PMS or other color system number by opening the color library and selecting one of the color books to match your color choices with.

Never use RGB or hexadecimal colors in your color story. Your color match numbers are designed to let your production factory know which color they need to dye your materials.

RGB is a digital color system, whereas the color match systems are CYMK and come with specially printed swatch books and chemical recipes that help a factory dye your materials the correct shade.

RGB stands for Red-Green-Blue and this is how the colors on your computer screen are created. CYMK stands for Cyan, Yellow, Magenta, and Black. The CYMK system is how colors are developed for products that are colored by using dye on a substrate (paper, textile).

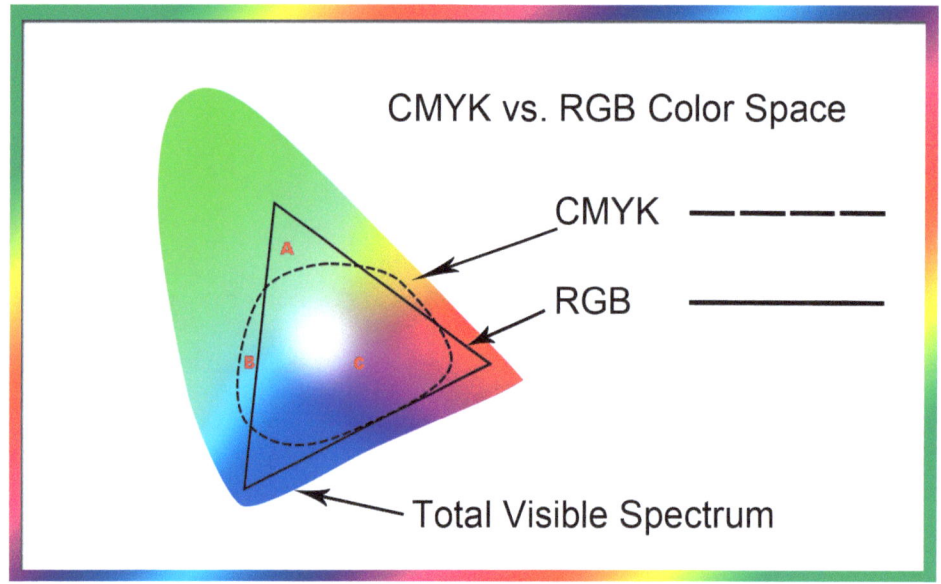

The two systems do not match exactly, and some colors in the RGB spectrum will not exactly match the CYMK color triangle, and vice versa.

There is currently no accurate RGB standard print out that a factory can use to develop a printed dye lot against, although there are several technologies in development that purport to match RGB to CYMK color match.

It is for this reason that you must always specify your colors using a CYMK color library numbering system such as that provided by the Pantone Color Match System.

In naming your colors, keep in mind that you can name colors anything you like, but in a real production setting, your colors will probably be presented to you by your art department. In a production setting, a single color will always keep exactly the same name no matter how many times it is reused.

This prevents confusion with the production team. However, for the sake of your portfolio, you can name the exact red with different names, since your collections you are developing for your visual story are not likely to be produced.

Your material selections and your trims may be placed onto the same image depending on how many materials and trims you are incorporating into your collection. You may also want to add any textile prints that you have developed.

Make sure you show your prints in color-ways, with every color used in each color-way properly broken out and labeled, just as you would send it out to a factory for reproduction. Presenting your prints in this way tells your viewer that you know how to communicate your prints and screens to your factories.

A color-way is a visually distinctive colored version of a style. Generally there are two-six unique color-ways per style; each color-way consists of a selection of colors/trims/prints. All styles that have the same colorway in a collection one will use some combination of the same predominant color(s).

Next you add in your fashion sketches. In general, you want to show your product in groupings of two-three outfits; for accessories it can range from one-two products up to 16 products on a page. Apparel is shown on a figure while accessories are usually shown by themselves.

Use the ghosted mood board as the background for your product groupings. You can also create a unique frame that helps anchor your product on the page. Never show your sketches floating on a plain white page with no frame. That is the hallmark of student work or worse, a hobbyist.

We will not cover the how-to's of fashion sketching, as this is something which is usually covered in one or more classes as part of your fashion design program. There are also several very good fashion sketching books you can refer to if you need more in-depth instruction on this matter. You can find those listed in the bibliography.

After your fashion sketches, you should add flats and technical specifications. In general, you can show all of your flats for the fashion groupings on a single page.

Do not be afraid to overlap them and arrange them attractively. Show your flats in color runs of different color-ways. This shows you understand the idea of designing a collection of products designed to be marketed as a group.

Technical specifications should be included in their entirety. If you have had experience developing trims or specifying hardware, you may also want to add the additional specifications for those as well. The idea is to show your audience that you are well rounded, and to give them an idea of your depth of experience and scope of talent.

Students starting out usually will not have trim or hardware specifications unless they have had an internship where they focused on these areas. As you become more experienced, you will have actual photographs and scans of trims you have developed which you can include with these tech packs as well.

A complete visual story will include everything from an initial mood or inspiration board through to the final technical manufacturing specifications. As a student or a new designer, you may not have all of the pieces to tell a full story.

At the bare minimum, you should have the mood board, color story, materials story, and design concepts. You may add additional supporting material such as technical specifications, especially if you intend to showcase your strong technical design skills.

Keep in mind that your visual story needs to both be able to stand on its own, and tell a story to the viewer, and it needs to allow you to actually talk through your motivation and intention for the collection.

The reason it needs to stand on its own merit is that you may be asked to send images to a recruiter or a human resource representative where you will not be present to offer your commentary about your visual story. Your viewer needs to be able to make sense out of your story.

On the other hand, when you do have a face-to-face meeting you want your visual story to be compelling enough that you can talk about your intended target market, how you think the collection will fit into that market, as well as some of the trends you are capitalizing on. In cases where you have more experience, and can talk about sales performance, you will definitely want to highlight the styles that sold well. If you have numbers or sales volume for your styles, your story becomes even more compelling.

Designing Collections

In design school, students customarily work on individual items rather than learning to design a complete collection. The final semester of a student's work will usually be highlighted by some version of the senior collection. For many students, this may be the first exposure they have to the process of designing a collection.

This is unfortunate because all aspects of the apparel industry work in a collection system. Regardless of whether you are designing apparel or footwear, accessories or home furnishings, designers must learn to think, design, and otherwise create products that work well as a collection.

The reason for this is that collections enable customers to purchase multiple products to create complete looks. By presenting a collection of styles that work well with one another, the customer is provided with a broader range of options that can lead to larger sales volume from the same customer on the same collection. As a designer, you want to be able to offer enough options to a customer that they will make multiple purchases out of the same collection.

Accessories designers are usually asked to create collections of products within the same class and category. So, for example, you may be asked to create a collection of casual ladies' shoes or a collection of men's performance gloves.

Smaller design houses may require an accessories designer to be able to design into multiple product classes (handwear, headwear, neckwear, footwear, and so on) whereas larger houses will segregate their designers into product classes.

As you begin assembling your portfolio, you will want to define what sort of work you wish to do. Do you want to design handbags and only handbags, or do you want a more diversified design career?

If you want to focus in only one product class, you would do well to showcase that product throughout your portfolio. You do run the risk of not having as many opportunities as a more diversified designer, but if you are really set on designing only shoes, then it is better to show just shoes in your portfolio.

There is an argument to be made that showing your portfolio to people who want you to design hats, when you don't want to design hats, would be a monumental waste of time for all parties. Only you can decide how you want to pursue your job search plan and intended career path.

In assembling your collections, try to design six-twelve pieces for each visual story. You can opt for the mixed product collection (handbags, shoes, belts) or all one product (shoes).

You can show the full collection on a single page, like a visual line sheet, or you can choose to display groupings of your product (two-three pieces) per page, or some combination thereof. Use the layout that makes the most sense to you and is most visually appealing.

Always remember, you are trying to convey to your viewer that you have the understanding of the industry and the skill set that will make you a valuable design asset. Showcasing your ability to design within the collection is a great start.

Process & Technique

A critical component of your portfolio is demonstrating that you have superior technique in your preferred area of design.

You can do this in one of several ways: first, you can actually create two-four technique pages, where you showcase specific sketch or technical techniques, such as latex, feathers, plaid/prints, fur, suede, metals, jewels, and so on.

Title the pages appropriately, and then place them at the front or the back of your portfolio, depending on where you want the emphasis to lie.

Alternately, you can highlight your versatility by creating collections that incorporate several of these techniques per collection. The danger of presenting your skills this way is that you may end up presenting collections that are very expensive to produce. This strategy is fine if you are pursuing work with a luxury brand, but be warned it may backfire if you are interviewing with a mid-priced brand.

If you are unclear about with whom you will be interviewing, it is a very good idea to use separate technique pages, and put them at the back of your portfolio. This also serves as a gauge of interest – if your viewer

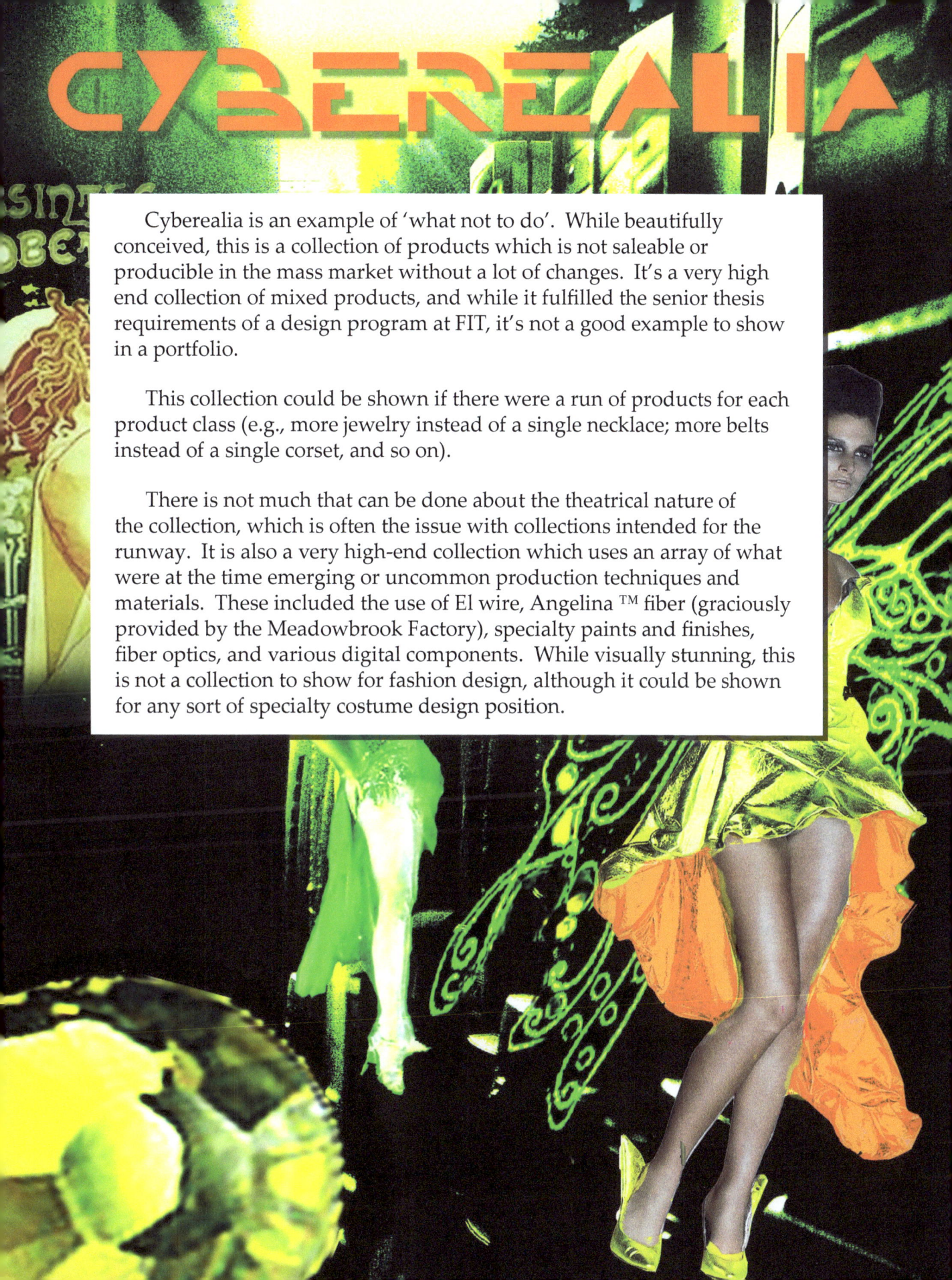

CYBEREALIA

Cyberealia is an example of 'what not to do'. While beautifully conceived, this is a collection of products which is not saleable or producible in the mass market without a lot of changes. It's a very high end collection of mixed products, and while it fulfilled the senior thesis requirements of a design program at FIT, it's not a good example to show in a portfolio.

This collection could be shown if there were a run of products for each product class (e.g., more jewelry instead of a single necklace; more belts instead of a single corset, and so on).

There is not much that can be done about the theatrical nature of the collection, which is often the issue with collections intended for the runway. It is also a very high-end collection which uses an array of what were at the time emerging or uncommon production techniques and materials. These included the use of El wire, Angelina ™ fiber (graciously provided by the Meadowbrook Factory), specialty paints and finishes, fiber optics, and various digital components. While visually stunning, this is not a collection to show for fashion design, although it could be shown for any sort of specialty costume design position.

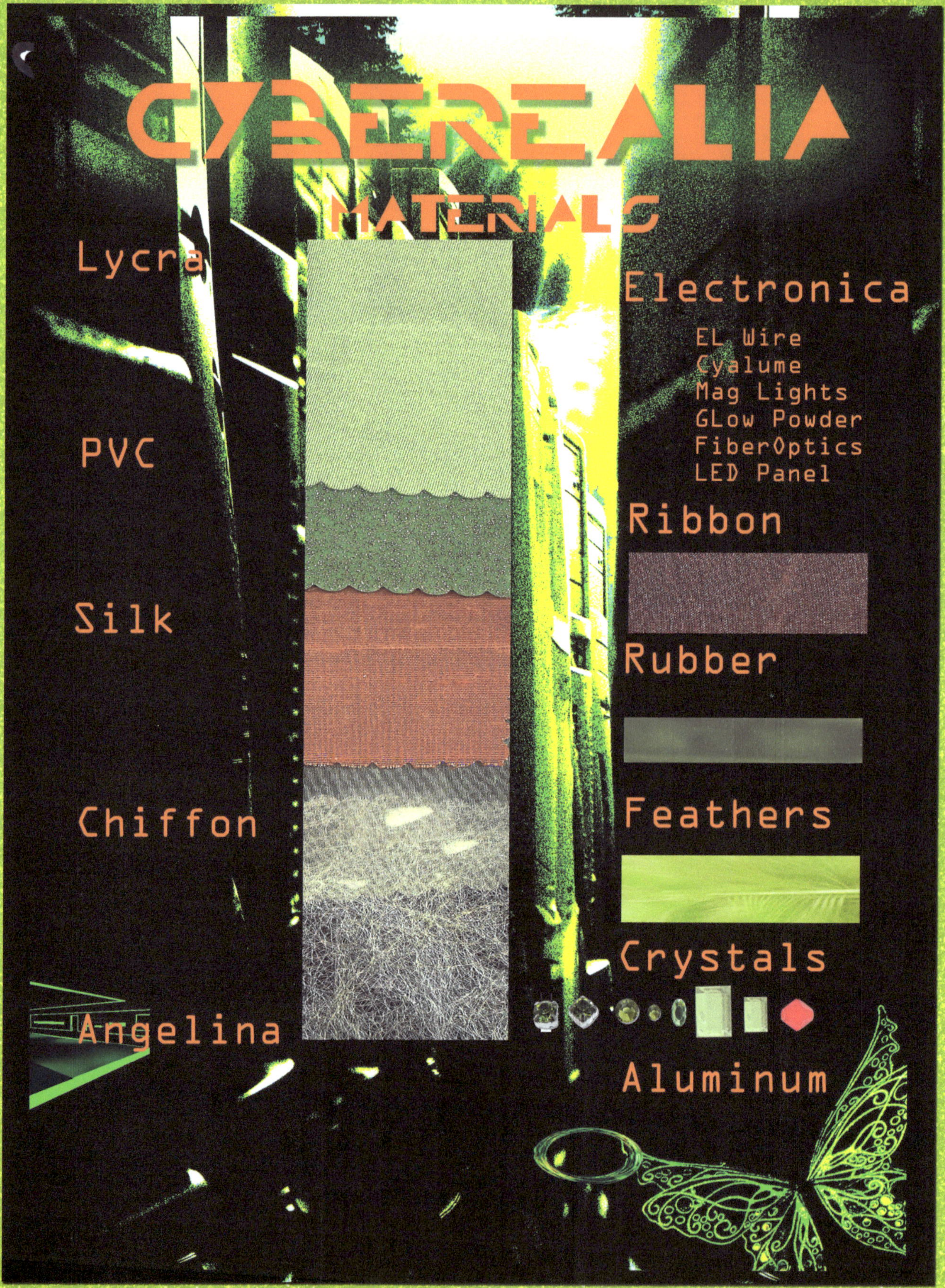

CYBEREALIA
MATERIALS

Lycra

PVC

Silk

Chiffon

Angelina

Electronica
EL Wire
Cyalume
Mag Lights
GLow Powder
FiberOptics
LED Panel

Ribbon

Rubber

Feathers

Crystals

Aluminum

stops before the technique pages, you have either overwhelmed them with too much material or your design sensibility isn't what they are looking for.

This leads us to the question of process. What is process, you ask, and why should you care about it?

Process is the pathway you follow with any creative endeavor, starting from the initial raw concepts through to the final output, whatever that may be. Showing your viewer that you understand how a design process works can help the interviewer have a better insight into your personal design process.

You should care about this because if your own design process is too far from what is followed by the design house with which you are interviewing, then even if they do hire you, you will experience the inevitable friction between your preferred and their required design process.

You can show process simply by creating one-two pages of simple thumbnail sketches, perhaps even incorporating a small flow cycle showing how you would have your product created (start with a thumbnail, move on the nicer fashion sketch, and then to a flat, and so on).

Remember, you are trying to show your viewer that you understand the process of how design works, not give them a complete collection.

You can do this with very simple rough pencil sketches worked up quickly. Scan the images and collage them nicely onto one or two pages, and make sure you put a title on the page.

Incorporate the process page(s) in the same area as the technique page(s) to create a comprehensive whole. Again, keep your audience in mind to assemble and place these pages, and keep in mind how they will work along with the other sections of your portfolio such as the media coverage and awards section.

Media Coverage & Awards

During the process of design school, hopefully you will have accumulated awards and possibly even some media coverage. This section is where you can really showcase any media coverage or awards your work received.

It isn't necessary to devote an entire page of your portfolio to each press mention or award you received.

Your press coverage, media mentions and awards are not the most important part of your book. Instead, collage your awards or press coverage on one or two pages. Use the headlines and titles of the print media, add screen shots of the web page or blog, web sites and other digital media, including video.

Use your resume to good effect, adding specific URLs, dates, and titles of any coverage or awards you may have won. Don't add your resume as a page in your portfolio. It will tend to change too frequently.

The idea is to tease your viewer and show them that you have received some level of critical acclaim. It's not necessary or desirable to include every award or mention you've ever received. In particular, as you become more experienced, you will want to drop your older awards, especially the ones you received while a student.

An experienced designer continuing to showcase student awards tells the viewer that the designer hasn't moved on with his or her career. Once a designer is out in the world, his or her work will sooner or later get selected for ad work - having ads showcasing your designs to support your work is far better than having a decades-old Dean's List commendation.

Supporting Cast

You may wish to add additional components to your portfolio and your job search such as digital media, catalogs, leave-behinds, trims, and so on. These components can be a critical component to help you stand out from the crowd.

Within the portfolio itself, you may wish to add catalogs or composed line sheets that are tipped in using document holders within the pertinent visual story. You may want to add a special material or trim page, where you mount the trims on heavy stock and use an acrylic cover sheet, which you can flip up to enable your viewer to feel the materials.

A new or emerging designer may have to create mockups of line sheets, which is still a good way to demonstrate her awareness of these documents.

With the many new digital prototyping services available, you can even showcase some of your textile prints, or add small hardware or other

prototype examples that can be added to your book easily.

You may also want to go high tech, and incorporate various sorts of new media. For example, you can easily create videos that can be shown on most mobile devices, including net books or portable DVD players.

You may also wish to create slide shows incorporating photographs of your work. Keep in mind; you can show a great deal of your work in a 2-minute video, plus you can incorporate voice over and music to set the mood.

You can also add other useful digital links, such as your blog, twitter handle, LinkedIn ID, and Facebook page, where you can show more of your work to recruiters or hiring agents. A word to the wise on social media: do not ever display anything that may make hiring you a questionable activity.

Please see the section on 'Beyond the Book' for suggested services and products if you wish to explore taking your portfolio beyond the ordinary.

Taking a Bow

Once you have completed all of the components for your portfolio, you still have one page left—the end page. This last page is an odd duck, literally, because it is the last page of the book, a single page, and the page that will be regarded the least and yet at the same time, looked at perhaps the most.

The reason it fits into all of these categories is that it is usually the last page your interviewer will stop on; you need to have something to let the viewer know they have come to the end of the book; and you cannot start anything new here, it must wrap up all of your talents and abilities into one neat tidy package, and hopefully, crown it with a pretty little bow.

We would like to say that after you had completed all of the exercises to complete your book, that the final page should be a simple slam-dunk. As you will see when you come to this page, it's not really as easy as that.

First of all, you have to decide what the last page needs to say, and then how to say it visually. Do you want your last page to reflect technical designer? Luxury designer? Trim designer?

Do you want to invite more conversation about your technique, or do you want to focus your interview on your creative abilities? Do you want to lead your interviewer to talk about things that may be outside of your current range of ability, but that you hope to learn or embark upon?

There is no right or wrong answer here, by the way. It really does depend on how you want to guide your interview and the subsequent discussion you will have with your interviewer after they have reviewed your book.

As your viewer rests her eyes on that last page, you should have something there that allows you to have one or more topics of conversation.

It is always tempting to slap a 'The End' title on the last page, but you will leave this tremendous opportunity for more involved discussion about your possible career with the organization that you are interviewing with.

So spend some time and think through what you really want to do (and don't just say get a job, because that is already pretty well assumed). And then create a strong, visual ending to your book that invites deeper discussion and may give you an opportunity to discuss at greater length a career, rather than just a job.

So what sort of endings might you add? For a technical designer, perhaps you might show a ghosted (30%) version of a fully exploded flat (a flat is a black line 2-D drawing of the design laid out 'flat' to show design details and measurements), with her name and blog or web site address.

A line designer may decide to sketch a gorgeous fashion sketch that showcases their work in a physical setting. A textile designer may opt to show his work in a whimsical setting like a quilt line, where each quilt block uses a different print.

There are several ways to showcase your work in a nontraditional manner that allows you the opportunity to talk about what you really want to do.

Are you visionary? Do you want to show this off using some new technologies out there? Showcase your future forward sensibilities by using some of the easy to use new technologies out there.

For example, you can create one or more QR codes (like a bar code that contains a lot of information, but can be read by many common mobile devices with a plug-in that allows the device to scan it).

Or maybe you could create a keyword cloud (see wordle.net) showing your skills using your skills as the keywords.

Get funky – you can play a bit here. Do you love unique and innovative materials? How about using lenticular or hologrammatic for your title? You could create a pop-up visual at the end (time consuming, but guaranteed to make you stick out positively).

Don't waste the last page because you got tired. Change it often, add to it, and take away from it. Keep it fresh and interesting. This way, you will always close your book, and your interview, on an interesting, upbeat note.

Chapter Five
Portfolio Etiquette

Chapter Five
Portfolio Etiquette

The etiquette of the portfolio is something every design student and aspiring designer should study and learn.

A casual viewer often won't have much concept of how much time and money you will have invested in developing your portfolio, and so they may ask you for images from your portfolio or a copy of it, simply because they liked how it went together. They think they are complimenting you (or your skill) and will not understand that they have committed a breach of etiquette.

For that matter, until you really begin developing your own professional portfolio, you won't understand why asking others for copies of their work is a major breach of etiquette.

Once you have invested sweat equity into your portfolio, it will become clear to you why you never ask for copies of images you see in someone else's portfolio; you don't ask for a copy of their portfolio; and you never ask if you can borrow it. It's impolite to say the least!

You may find people within the industry who will ask to have copies of your work. These may include potential employers, headhunters, potential educational opportunities, or other designers.

If a potential employer is asking for copies of your work, they may be trying to find out how naive, or how desperate, you are.

Headhunters, or employment agencies, will often want to keep 2-3 digital copies of your work on hand so they can send them to potential employers.

Educators will ask for student portfolios of your work if you are applying to their school; other designers may ask because they don't know better, or if they do, they may not care how rude it is.

How you choose to respond to requests for your work will depend on the relationship you have with the person asking for it, the nature of the work they are asking for, and why they are asking for it. Let's get into the specifics of etiquette for your portfolio for these different classes of people.

Presenting to Educators

Your earliest experience in presenting your work will almost certainly be to an educator. When you apply to design school, you will be asked to develop some sort of portfolio to show to the admissions committee.

Usually, the educational institutions have specific projects they want you to create following their guidelines, which are required to be collated and presented to them in a standard format they have decided is most suitable to them.

Regrettably, not one of these projects will be the same; all of the schools will have their own unique projects they want you to address, and none of them will follow the same requested format.

They will almost all, however, require that you produce some form of portfolio to show your work, and they will want to see a visual story developed for them with their project as the topic.

It is going to be assumed that you are creative. This will hopefully be presented in your work. What is also assumed is that you will take direction from the admissions committee and produce a project for them following their exact instructions.

This is an important point to make. Exceptionally talented individuals abound in this industry. Individuals who refuse to take direction will have a short career unless they have the ability to attract venture capital to develop their own apparel line.

Having the discipline to follow the design program's specific instructions will make a favorable impression on the admissions committee, to which you may be required to present in person.

While you are waiting for your call, practice presenting your portfolio to your family or friends. Even having 2-3 run-throughs with your portfolio will help you think about what you want to say about it. Knowing you can present your work with authority, and minimal ums and ya-knows will do wonders for your confidence.

So what sorts of things should you say about your work? That depends very much on how the design school has described their required project. If they talk about line or silhouette, you should call out how you used line or silhouette to good effect in your project. If there is a specific topic you are required to design with, then talk about how your project focuses on that topic.

Hopefully you will be one of the lucky ones chosen for that personal interview, and you will be able to take your carefully crafted admissions portfolio with you.

While you are waiting to be called in for your interview, remove your admissions portfolio from any carrying case, handbag or tote you may have stashed it in for transportation.

Have it ready on your lap, with your resume or any additional application material placed between the last page and the back cover where you have quick access.

If you have created a special diorama or display, then just place any additional paperwork on top of the diorama, facedown. Clip your papers together - there is nothing worse than dropping them as you stand up and try to recover them, and your poise, at the same time. Remember, you want to convey quiet confidence in your design ability.

It is hard to do that when you are scrambling around on your hands and knees, trying to pick up loose papers.

Put all extra items in your handbag or portfolio case, so you have your hands free to deal with your portfolio. You will usually need to bring any personal items that you have brought (like your handbag) with you into your interview, so dress and plan accordingly.

When you are called in, take a deep breath and smile. Trust us on this one; it will help you get through your interview. Stand up and shift your portfolio to your left hand and arm. In the U.S., you shake hands with your right hand if your interviewer offers to shake your hand. Otherwise, just smile and sit down where you are told to sit.

Since this is a book about how you need to develop and present your portfolio, we'll skip all the possible interview questions (there are lots of great books out there about interviewing, pick up a couple for good advice). We are focusing on your portfolio.

If you are seated at a table, place your portfolio or display in front of you. Don't fidget with it, and don't open it. Usually, there will be some paperwork—which may include the papers you have placed at the back of your portfolio.

You will specifically be invited to present to your audience, at which point, you do one of two things: rotate your portfolio to face your interviewer, or, you simply open the portfolio's cover.

What you do next is determined by where your interviewer(s) are located. If there is only one, or two, and they are seated with you, then you can simply open your book and begin. If they are seated across from you or along the side of the table, rotate the book first, and then open the cover.

Wait and make sure everyone is paying attention. Then begin presenting. The interviewer may ask questions as you go along, but in general, they will let you present your project to them as you see appropriate.

When you are done with your presentation, you can close your portfolio as a visual signal that you have nothing more to add or simply stop on your last page, which hopefully will be a powerhouse design.

Your interviewers may ask to see your book, in which case, hand it over and be ready to answer questions. Depending on how the admissions committee works, you may be asked to leave your portfolio with them, or, you may be asked to send it in to them in advance.

This is one of the only times in your life that you should simply smile and say yes.

Student work, even if very good, is still just student work. By the time you get done with your actual degree, your work, and your professional portfolio, will be so much stronger. In any event, you kept a copy of your admissions portfolio at home, with the rest of your projects (remember?)

It is uncommon for an admissions committee to ask you to leave your portfolio (they don't have space to store it, for one thing), but there will always be the one exception to any rule.

Be prepared for anything to happen in an educational portfolio review. This may include having the educator make disparaging remarks about your ability, your work, or even your outfit to having them stop you mid-way through and start talking about what you will need to do when admitted.

The key here is to stay flexible and simply roll with whatever is presented to you as long as it doesn't carry overtones of racism, sexism, or other forms of biased behavior. In such cases, you are well within your rights to simply stand up, thank your interviewer for their time, and leave.

This is a book about your portfolio, but it is important to remember, design school is about your ability to get trained to enter the apparel industry. You are interviewing the school as much as they are reviewing your abilities. It's not likely you'll be successful in an organization where you feel uncomfortable.

Once you have been admitted to design school, you will also be asked to present to your professors and instructors from time-to-time. Sketching and portfolio development classes are two obvious cases where you will be required to present your current work in an actual portfolio, but you should get in the habit of documenting all of your projects for all of your classes using a student portfolio.

The reason for this is that you may decide to create a visual story using one of the projects, and having your pictures, yield sheets, sketches, and so on, all gathered together will make this a much easier process.

In presenting to your current instructors, you should be prepared to present one-on-one with them. Complete your assignments all the way through, and follow their advice and specific direction. Design instructors who ride you hard usually know what all design industry personnel have also learned: it's a tough industry, and slackers are the first to get cut from payroll in downtime, and the last to get hired.

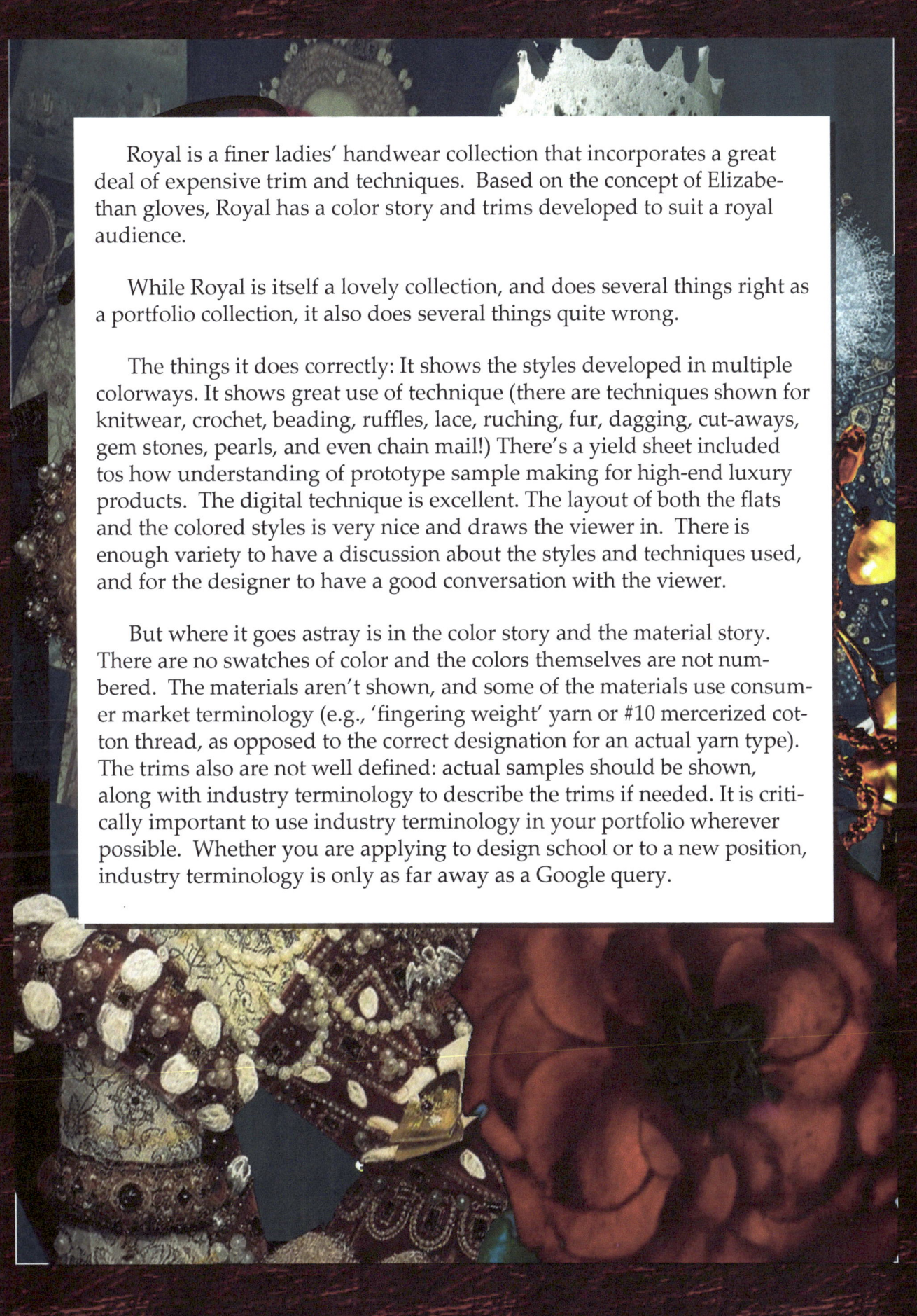

Royal is a finer ladies' handwear collection that incorporates a great deal of expensive trim and techniques. Based on the concept of Elizabethan gloves, Royal has a color story and trims developed to suit a royal audience.

While Royal is itself a lovely collection, and does several things right as a portfolio collection, it also does several things quite wrong.

The things it does correctly: It shows the styles developed in multiple colorways. It shows great use of technique (there are techniques shown for knitwear, crochet, beading, ruffles, lace, ruching, fur, dagging, cut-aways, gem stones, pearls, and even chain mail!) There's a yield sheet included tos how understanding of prototype sample making for high-end luxury products. The digital technique is excellent. The layout of both the flats and the colored styles is very nice and draws the viewer in. There is enough variety to have a discussion about the styles and techniques used, and for the designer to have a good conversation with the viewer.

But where it goes astray is in the color story and the material story. There are no swatches of color and the colors themselves are not numbered. The materials aren't shown, and some of the materials use consumer market terminology (e.g., 'fingering weight' yarn or #10 mercerized cotton thread, as opposed to the correct designation for an actual yarn type). The trims also are not well defined: actual samples should be shown, along with industry terminology to describe the trims if needed. It is critically important to use industry terminology in your portfolio wherever possible. Whether you are applying to design school or to a new position, industry terminology is only as far away as a Google query.

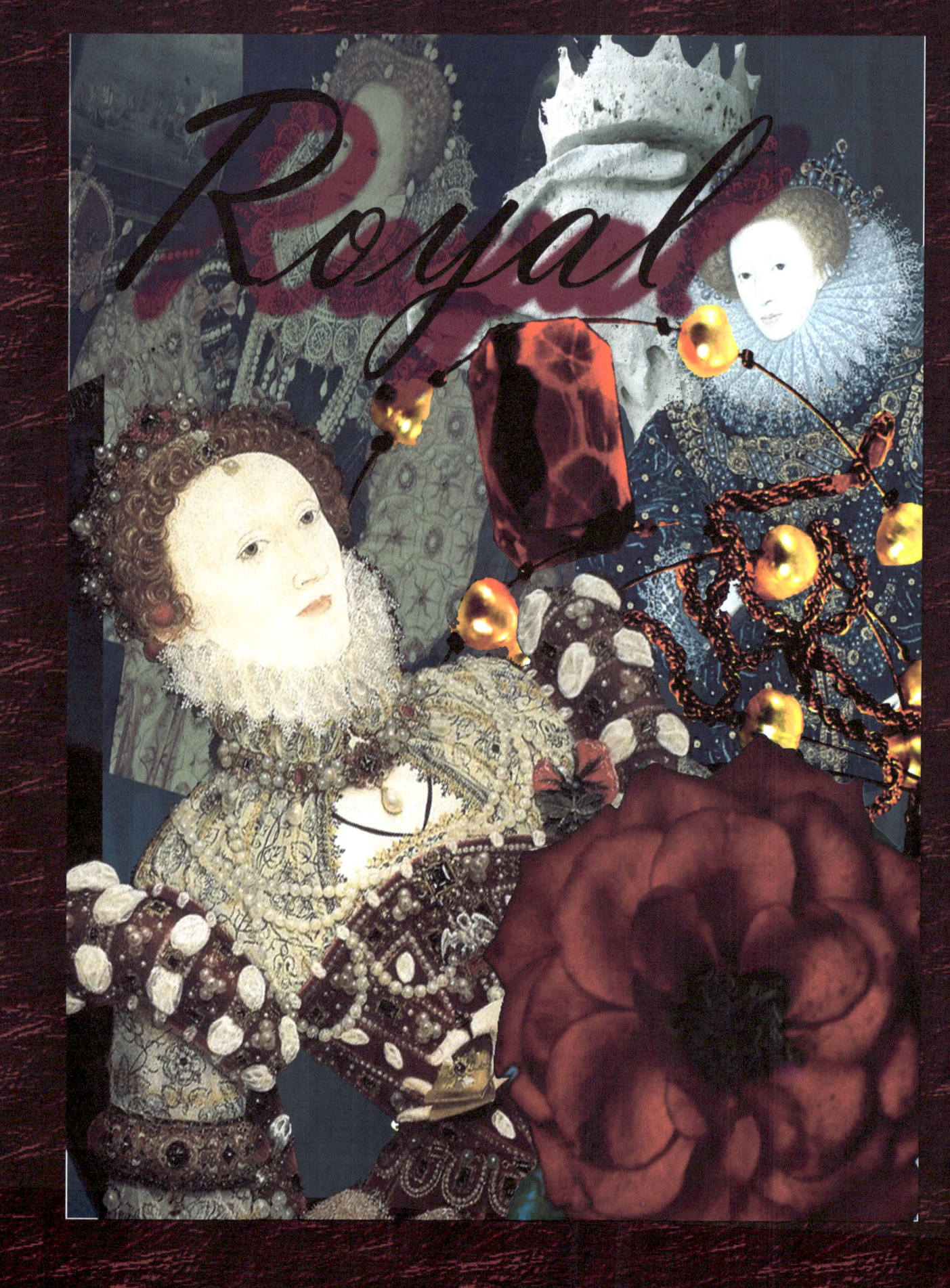

Royal

Materials & Trims

Materials
Moleskin Doubleknit
Lame Acrylic Singleknit
Tricot Nylon Sheer Singleknit
Fingering Weight Acrylic Yarn
#10 Mercerized Cotton Thread

Trims
Heat set Pearls & Crystals
Faux Opal Cabochons
Full Hole Faux Pearls
Long Nap Single Knit Faux Fur
Venice Lace Motifs
Alencon Border Lace
#5 Rayon Thread
#10 Cotton Thread Irish Lace Crochet Motifs
Faux Pearl Buttons
Acrylic Rings

Color Story
Merlot
Thames Brown
Queen's Gold
Puritan Black
African Ivory

Yield Sheet for Fabric

Name: Leicester
Style #: Royal-05
Season: Autumn 2007
Description: Moleskin doubleknit fitted ladies' glove with French thumb and hand-stitched gouches; scalloped cuff trimmed with faux pearl cabochons
Colorways: Thames Brown & Queen's Gold; African Ivory & Queen's Gold; Merlot & Queen's Gold; Puritan Black & African Ivory

Pattern Piece Name of Piece	Dimensions Length	Width	Area Subtotal	# of pieces	Area Total (Sq. Inches)
Glove Body	15.00 inches	9.50 inches	142.50 si	2	285.00
Thumb Gusset	4.38 inches	3.50 inches	15.31 si	2	30.63
Fourchettes	6.25 inches	0.88 inches	5.47 si	6	32.81
			Total Square Inches:		348.44
			35% Waste		121.95
			Total Square Inches:		470.39
			Total Square Feet:		3.27
			1 yard, 54" wide	13.50 sf	
			Yardage =		0.242 yards

Pattern Piece Name of Piece	Dimensions Length	Width	Area Subtotal	# of pieces	Area Total (Sq. Inches)
Cuff	5.50 inches	12.50 inches	68.75 si	2	137.50
Cuff Lining	5.50 inches	12.50 inches	68.75 si	2	137.50
			Total Square Inches:		275.00
			35% Waste		96.25
			Total Square Inches:		371.25
			Total Square Feet:		2.58
			1 yard, 54" wide	13.50 sf	
			Yardage =		0.191 yards

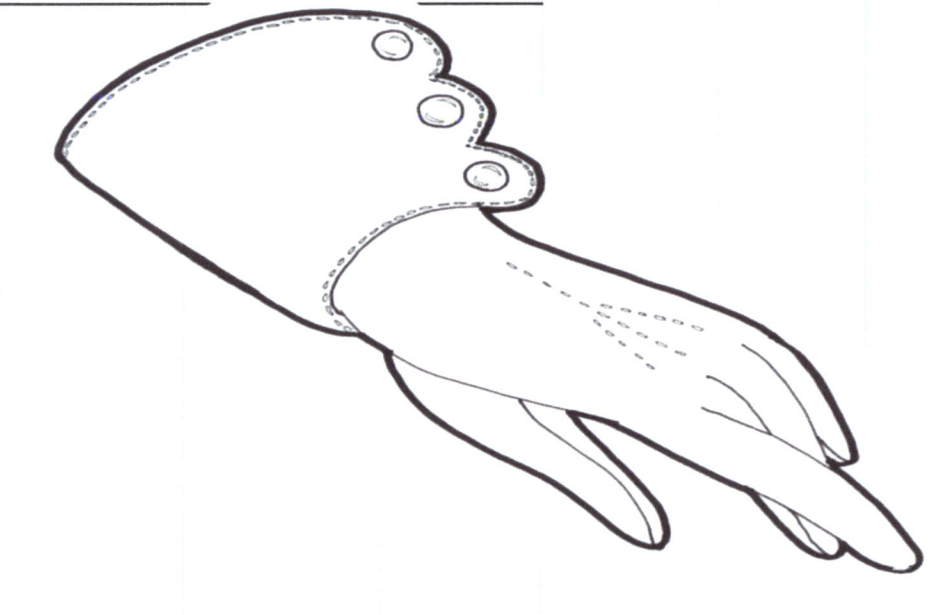

If you do not work at your craft, it will show. Your instructors teach many students and they can tell if you have done your work or if you thought a last-minute sketch hastily shoved into your portfolio would actually pass their review. Listen actively to their feedback in reviewing your work.

Instructors all have different personalities, and some may be gruff while others are warm, but in the end they are all teaching design because they love design and they love to teach. No one teaches design because of the incredible financial rewards.

Keep this in mind when you are receiving feedback—even if it doesn't seem like it, your design teachers actually do want you to succeed and they are pushing you because they know you'll need it when you go out to get your first job.

Presenting to Your Peers

In design school and beyond, you will have an opportunity to present your portfolio, projects and designs to your peers, first as classmates, and later in networking and design workshops.

One of the things you will need to learn early on is to develop a bit of a calloused skin with regards to critique, because your entire design career will consist of either being critiqued or critiquing. Keep in mind when presenting to your peers that a wide range of emotions will motivate their comments.

Some of your classmates will be genuinely interested in helping you advance, while others will be motivated by envy. You need to be able to assess and recognize what is motivating your peer if you ask for a review of your work from one.

In general, having a peer review your work will not be as helpful as you may think. Unless you ask a classmate who is both ahead of you in your program, and who has exceptional abilities him or herself, the feedback you get will be mixed and of variable quality. Take that into consideration in evaluating their feedback.

That said, practicing the process of presentation with your peers is a very good idea. Making mistakes and fumbling in front of your peers is better than making mistakes in front of an audience that really matters, such as a recruiter.

Likewise, getting used to hearing a reviewer be utterly dismissive of your work is also very helpful, because you will have had the experience in a situation where the only damage that may be done is some wounded feelings.

A common type of peer presentation is the dreaded group project. Group projects are the bane of every design student's existence—even if you select friends with whom you think you will be able to really work well, invariably you discover that your BFF may have other ideas about what constitutes a good presentation.

Nevertheless, your ability to work with the group that you have either gathered or been assigned to will be reflected in your final set of presentation boards. These boards will hopefully be high quality and capable of being incorporated into your first draft of a professional portfolio.

In making this sort of presentation, which will usually be of a single design group or collection, keep in mind that everyone will need to talk about the work as a team effort. While one member of your team will be the lead spokesperson, all team members will need to contribute to discussion and presentation of at least one design or design group.

Your team will be presenting from a central location, usually the front of the classroom, and usually using large presentation boards. All team members should stay to one side of the boards, so that your audience can easily see the topics under discussion.

As each team member's turn arrives, they should move closer to the board so that they can point out areas of interest to the audience.

It's important to practice this kind of presentation. You never know when you may be called on to present in this way (to design directors, venture capitalists, investors, product managers, merchandisers, sales teams, or any of the other audiences out there). Learn how to present your design concepts to your peers and make your mistakes there. Knowing how to stand and speak well will help you sell your design ideas to your audience, and this ultimately is why you need to learn to present these design ideas out of your portfolio.

You will find that having presented to your peers in this way will make presenting to other audiences much easier. And occasionally, you will find you even get good feedback from your classmates about how to better present to them.

And finally, make sure you get high-quality prints of the boards to include in your portfolio. You will definitely want to have them.

Presenting to Recruiters

Another sort of portfolio presentation you can expect to make is presenting your portfolio, and by extension, yourself, to an employment recruiter.

Employment recruiters, by and large, want to know a few select facts: they want to know that, first of all, you actually have a portfolio.

Secondly, they want to get a sense of what types of skills that you have—whether your skills are stronger as a technical designer or as a line builder; if you know how to use computer programs, and if so, which ones; and what types of products you have experience in designing.

Recruiters have one or more employment vacancies they are trying to fill for their customers, which are usually the design houses you want to work with.

More often than not, they are experienced in human resources but not in design, but this does not mean they don't know what they are looking at, or what they are looking for.

Remember, they look at many portfolios from applicants every day and they, more than anyone, will have a good sense of what types of skills are most desirable, and how to best showcase your portfolio to get a good position.

Do not be afraid to ask them their opinion about your book. They want to have qualified candidates to present to their customers. And while they aren't working for you, they do have the ability to work on your behalf, since placing you means they get paid and if they place you it's likely you will maintain a relationship with them.

What makes presenting your portfolio to a recruiter challenging as a student or recent graduate is that you likely haven't gotten a lot of experience in any one area.

The student work you have done will be largely self-directed and chosen, which means that you probably don't have collections that were clearly designed for a particular trend or a brand.

The quality of the work reflects your inexperience, including the fact you have to invent so much of the detail of a collection instead of having actual factory specifications that you may have sent out to get a product produced. You won't (in general) have ads or photography of your work.

Nevertheless, you still need to be able to present high-quality work and talk about the collection as though you worked with a team in developing your ideas. This is where previous practice with your teachers or with other designers can be a tremendous help.

Recruiters largely won't have time to give you substantive feedback. They make money by placing as many people as possible, and if you aren't a strong candidate, they likely won't spend a great deal of time on your book or your presentation.

They will flip through your book quickly; rarely will they linger over any particular image or story.

If they see something they like, they may call other associates in to talk to you about the story or product and to confer about position openings they may have. You will find presenting to a recruiter to be a very fast-paced experience.

Be ready in advance and have your portfolio out, on your lap, in the waiting room. Don't make the recruiter wait while you dig your resume and portfolio out.

Have them ready so you can use the brief opportunity they are giving you to maximum advantage.

A recruiter may ask you to send themtwo-three digital images of your best work. Sometimes they may even tell you which images to send them. The simple answer to this request is yes, as soon as I get to my computer.

Werd!

Werd! Is a boy's performance handwear collection designed for large retailers. While all of the styles from this collection were sampled, not all went on to production for various reasons. Three of the styles shown here sold more than $1 million each, one style sold 1 million units, and three styles sold more than 1/3 million units each.

The Werd! Collection is shown in an expurgated form in order to incorporate a tech pack. The color story is not shown here, for example, and the materials are not shown in a fully blown out materials page. This is because what really makes this collection are the trims and the prints, which are shown.

The flats are also not shown and the style numbers are not included here. In general, with a collection like this, the style number would also be the SKU number used by the purchaser.

The tech pack included incorporates many pages to get a single glove produced. As you can see, there are extensive notes about the materials and production techniques, as well as sizing information and color ways.

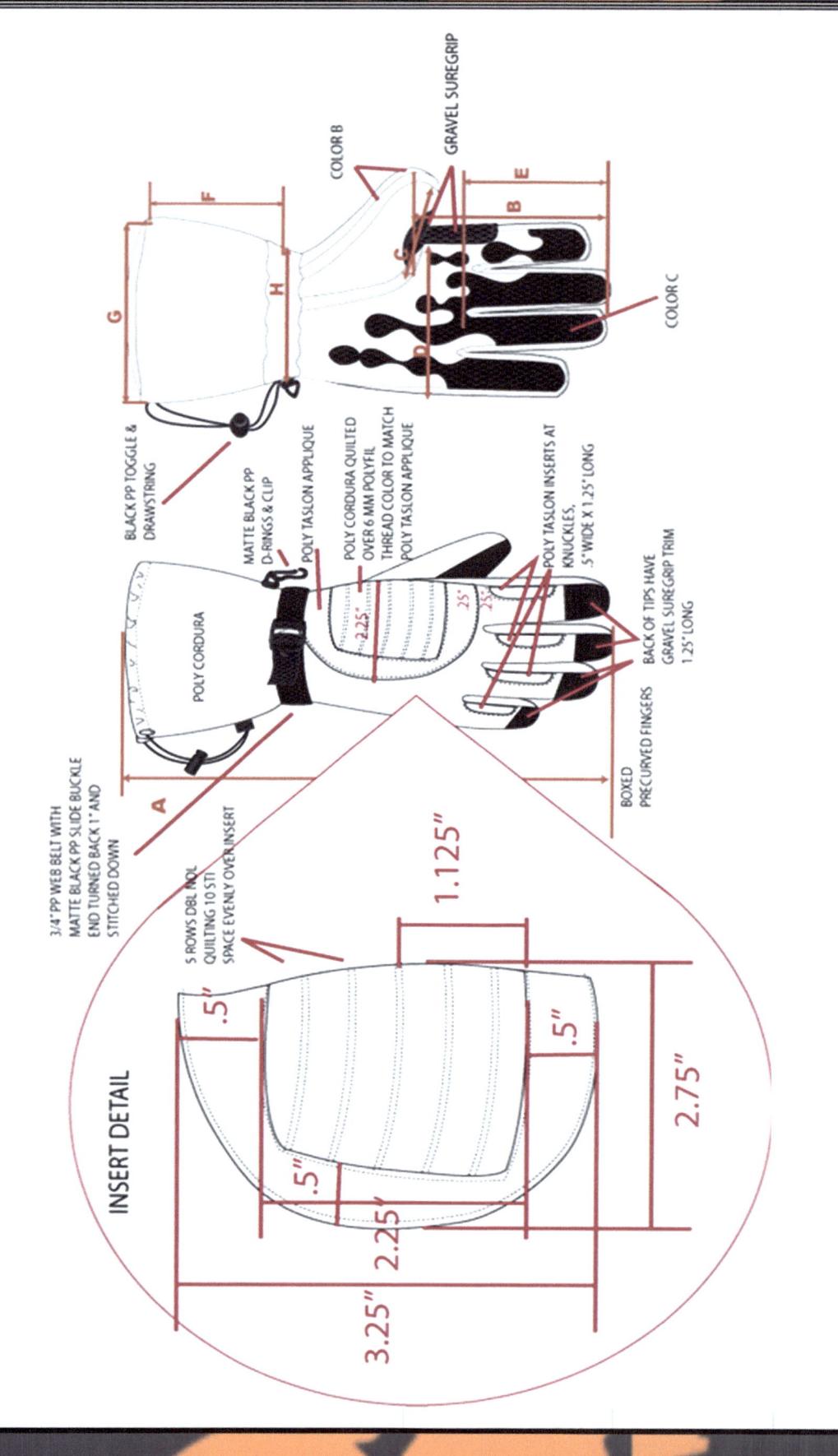

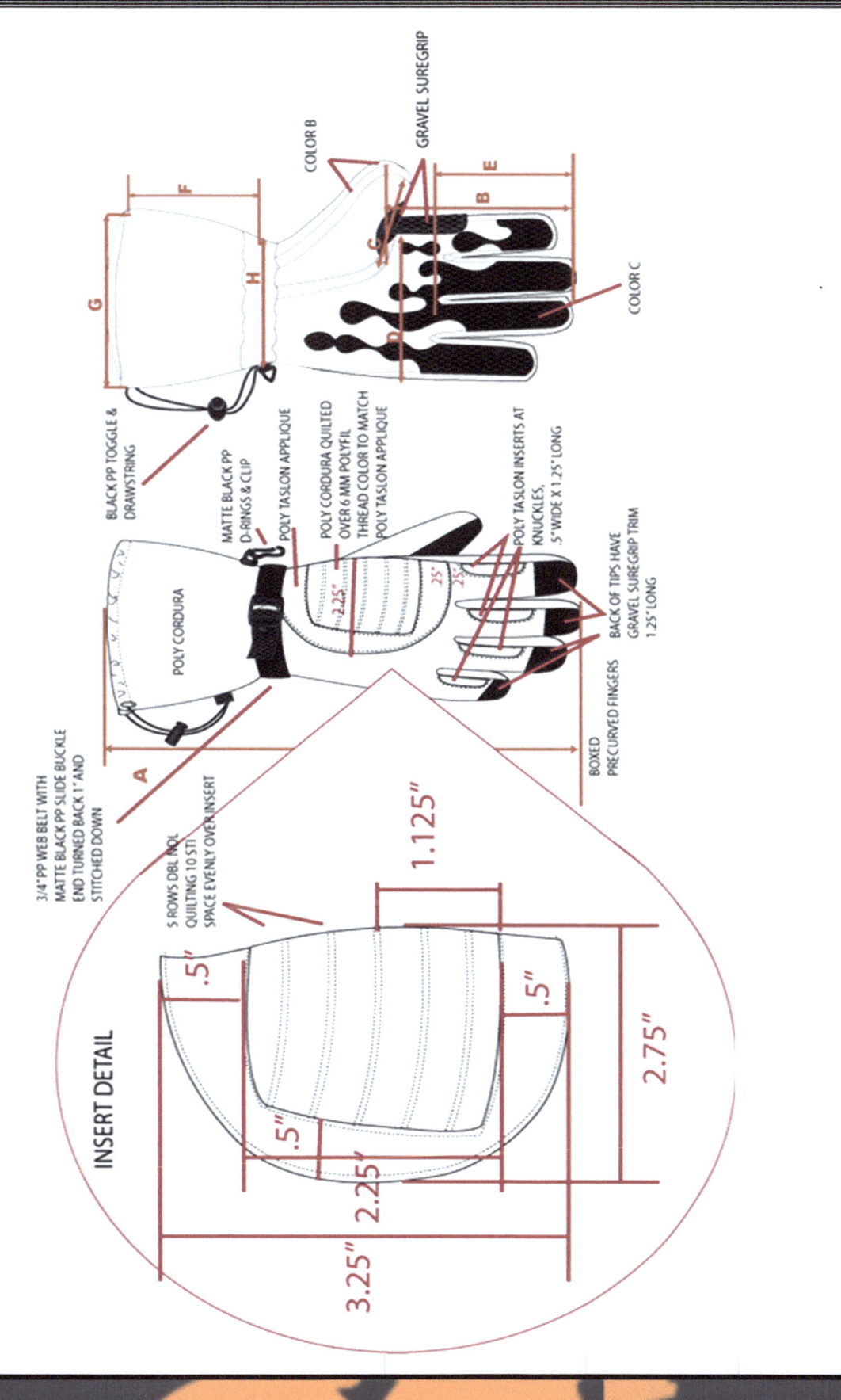

SPECIFICATION ARTWORK - FALL
SKI GLOVES

| DATE ISSUED: | 9/22/2006 | REF. / DEV. #: | 97B70017-1 | SAMPLE SIZE: | BOYS SZ 8-10 |

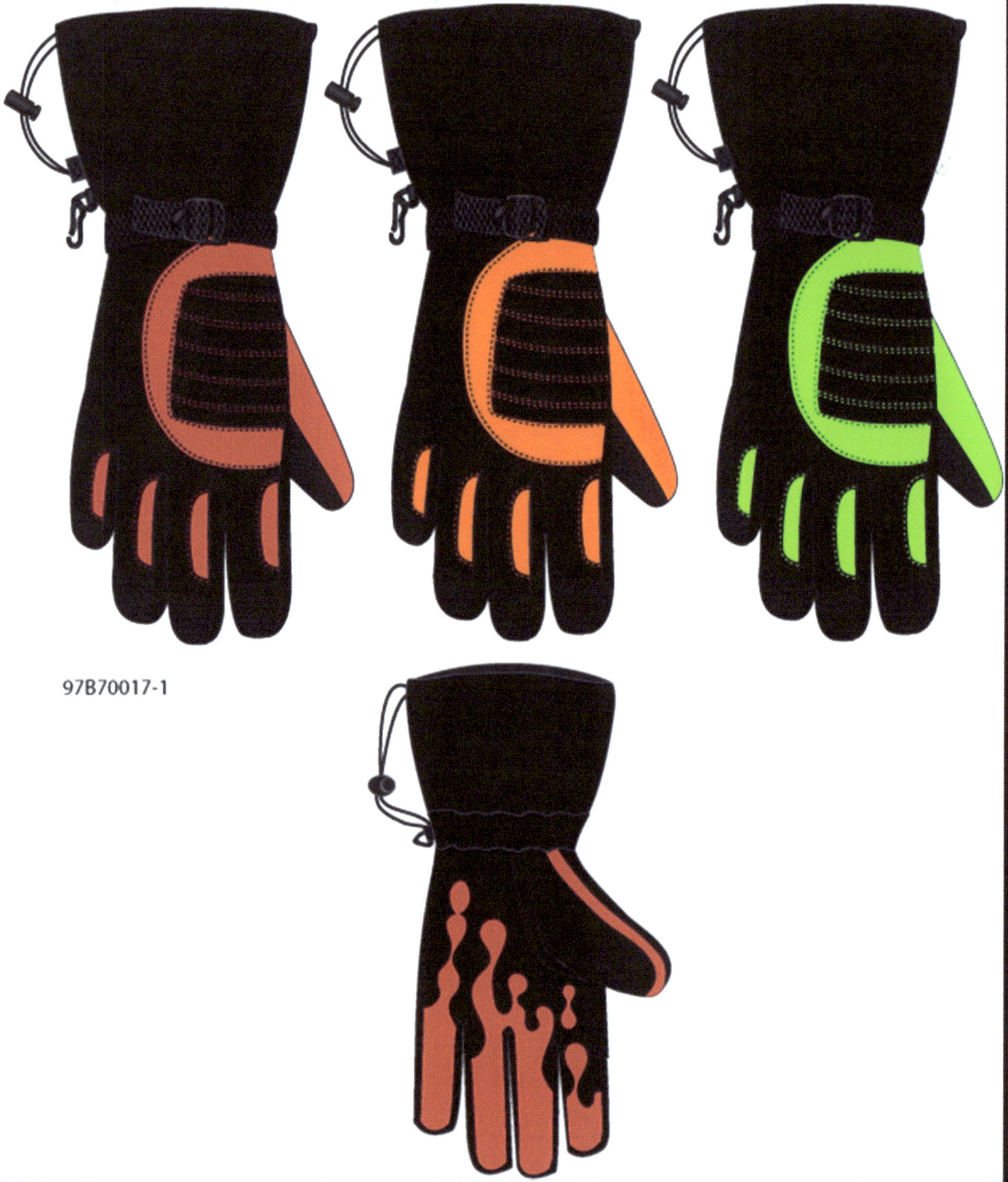

97B70017-1

SPEC SHEET DIMENSIONS - FALL   SKI GLOVES

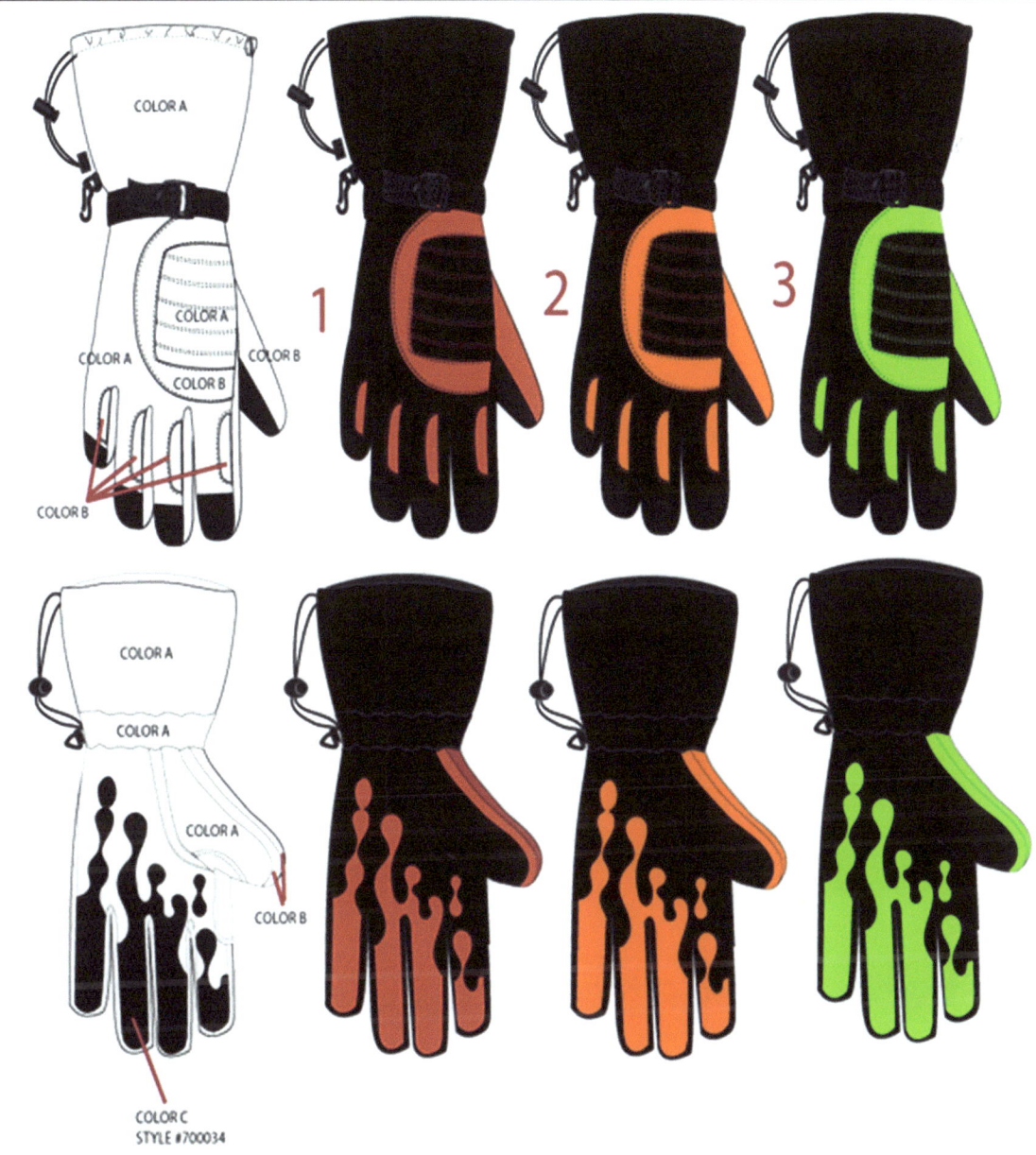

	POLY CORDURA #1080	POLY TASLON 210D	STYLE #12-B	THREAD FOR QUILTING CORDURA INSERT			
	(A)	(B)	(C)	(D)	(E)	(F)	(G)
C/W 1	BLACK SOOT 210131	CLASSIC RED 20345	CLASSIC RED 20345	CLASSIC RED 20345			
C/W 2	BLACK SOOT 210131	TANGERINE 16-1364	TANGERINE 16-1364	TANGERINE 16-1364			
C/W 3	BLACK SOOT 210131	EURO-FRESH 376-C	EURO-FRESH 376-C	EURO-FRESH 376-C			

ART PITCH SHEET - FALL   SKI GLOVES

4 1/4"

5 1/2"

C/W #1:
CLASSIC RED
#20345

C/W #2:
TANGERINE
16-1364

C/W #3:
EURO-FRESH
376C

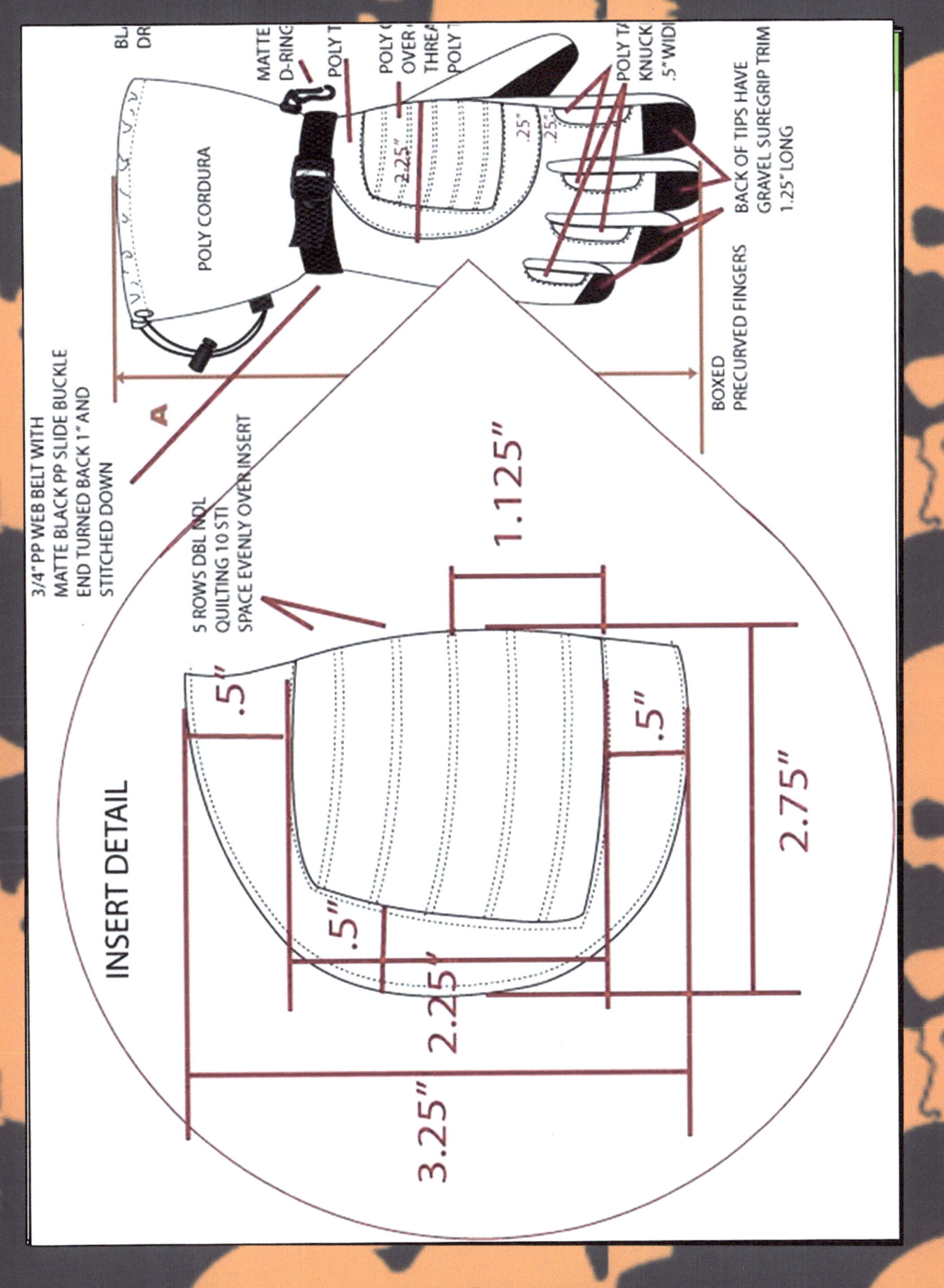

And then do it. The recruiter may use those images internally, to append to your resume or they may forward them on to be reviewed by their customer, the design house. While you have no control over how these images will be used, if you refuse to send them, odds are good that you will not be considered further.

You may also present your portfolio to recruiters at career fairs. Earlier in this book, we discussed how a smaller portfolio is better at these events.

If you have an opportunity to interview at one of these events, you will quickly find that the smaller portfolio will save your back and arms as you stand in lines that can be up to two hours long as you wait to meet a hiring representative face-to-face.

In general, you will be meeting human resources representatives rather than actual bosses, so this is just a first of several steps you will need to make before you get to meet with the person who you (hopefully) will actually be working with.

Have your portfolio ready to hand to the recruiter at these events. They may or may not ask to see it; first they'll ask for your resume and ask you what types of positions you may be interested in.

Hopefully, you will have done your homework about the company and you will have some idea about the kinds of products they create, so that you can ask sensible questions about how they handle designer and their designers.

Recruiters will be more forgiving than if you haven't done your homework—to some extent—but it really is a good idea to at least look at the web site of a company before you go stand on its recruitment line.

If a recruiter is even reasonably interested in you, they will ask to see your book. Have it ready, and hand it to them so that the bottom of the book is facing them. This way all they have to do is balance your book and flip through it, as opposed to turning it around. Also, remember how we said you need a good presentation system?

This is where it will shine—make sure you don't have loose papers in your portfolio, and above all, whittle it down to the best of the best. Recruiters at these events are inundated with applicants. They won't have time to go all the way through your book, so don't make them wade through the visual version of *War and Peace*.

Plus, your back and shoulders will thank you for it—you can safely expect to spend several hours at such an event; especially if there is a particular company in which you are very interested.

Don't be offended if they flip through your book rather quickly. The best you can hope for at these events are for them to put you into the follow up stack—they won't have the time or the space to do an in-depth interview with you, so keep your expectations reasonable.

If they tell you have a nice style but not what they are looking for, don't even think about a drama fit. Save the attitude for people who care, like your family—because the recruiter, whom you are in the process of seriously offending, will not only not care but also will quickly black list you if you pull any sort of drama at a job fair.

Thank them for their time, and move on to the next recruiter. Job fairs are a numbers game. They need to see a lot of applicants, and you need to see a lot of recruiters.

Interview Etiquette

Interview etiquette goes a bit beyond portfolio design, but we are including this section because it can be critically important to your career aspirations. Avoiding these mistakes and pitfalls as you present your portfolio may mean the difference between a job and no job. So here goes, some of the more important interview etiquette pointers.

1. Dress appropriately, yes! Know the brand you will be interviewing with and make plans to dress in a manner that suggests your design abilities will complement the brand. Never dress more casually than your interviewer. If you are attending a job fair, or any other mixed function, wear something middle of the road but with a certain level of flair.

Watch your necklines—cleavage is not appropriate at a job interview. Make sure your hosiery has no runs and your make up is on correctly. Polish your shoes. Wear clean clothes. Don't carry your beat up backpack—buy or borrow one that is in better shape. This is an appearance driven industry, so make sure you make the effort to look good.

Spring Romance

Spring Romance is a Spring/Summer ladies' headwear collection designed for the mass market. While this collection was never sold, it is similar to collections I designed in the past for big box retailers.

Note how the colors are both seasonally and gender appropriate: it uses pinks and teals, with soft tans and ecru. The materials are also seasonally appropriate: straws and cottons. Note how detailed the material specifications are.

The print chosen for this collection is an all-over rose print, reflecting the Spring Romance theme. This collection varies a bit in that it shows the simple pencil sketches, which move directly to a 3D model.

The collection was created using Black Dress Technology's Black Dress Design Studio, which enables designers to quickly and easily develop their styles as 3D models while at the same time creating their detailed technical specification package.

Spring 2010

Spring Romance

Rose Pink	PMS 671
Delicate	PMS 566
Dawn	PMS 7499
Precious	PMS 688
White	PMS WHITE
Mist	PMS 421
Passionate	PMS 676
Seacrest	PMS 562
Sunrise	PMS 7503
Wineberry	PMS 690
Soot Black	PMS BLACK

Spring 2010

Spring Romance

100% Cotton Duck
10 oz. 54/56

100% Natural Wheat Straw
Untreated

100% Polypropylene
4-Strand Braid

100% Cotton Lining
Lightweight 54/56

100% Polyester
Nonwoven Interfacing

Spring 2010

2. Personal hygiene, yes! Shower and use deodorant. Use minimal (if any) perfume. Allergies to scents are common these days, and you do not want your interviewer to have an allergic reaction to you…you will not get the job if she does. Comb your hair. No tears in your clothing, no matter how trendy distressing may be.

3. Eating and drinking, no! Do not chew gum or eat candy in your interview. For that matter, unless it is an interview conducted at a meal, don't eat anything at all. If you are the clumsy sort, do not accept their offer for liquid refreshments.

It's usually a de facto offer anyway, and you'd do better to not have anything around that you might knock over. If you get parched while interviewing, bring in your own bottled water to drink and keep it capped and off your interviewer's desk.

4. Mobile devices, no! Turn off your cell phones and other portable devices. DO NOT EVER MAKE OR TAKE A CALL IN AN INTERVIEW. Likewise, no texting. Turn it off, put it away, the world is not going to collapse if you can't text your BFF for an hour. Really. It won't.

5. Questions, yes! When they ask you if you have any questions, make sure you do. At least one, maybe even two or three. Otherwise they will think you aren't interested in the company, the job, or even them. People like to hire people who are interested in them

6. Some generic personal habits: Do not spit. If you sneeze, hankie please. Keep your body byproducts within your body while in the interview. If you are sick, postpone the interview – vomiting in the interviewer's office is not the way to get a job nor is it how you wish to be remembered.

7. Check in politely at the receptionist desk. Don't irritate the receptionist—that's just plain foolhardy to make an enemy there. S/he likely isn't paid enough to put up with some unemployed designer's diva drama, so behave and play nicely.

8. Absolutely no diva attitude unless you truly are a premium, top-of-the-field designer, in which case, why are you reading this book?

9. Meal interviews: try to avoid these. If you get stuck with one, eat first; you won't have time to eat and answer interview questions. If you do end up at such an interview, you will be expected to order something,

so keep it middle of the road. Ordering the most expensive item on the menu isn't going to impress anyone, especially since you aren't going to have time to eat it anyway.

Use your best table manners. Napkin on lap. Chew with your mouth closed. Get your elbows off the table. Don't reach across the table for salt, bread, or anything else. Move slowly so that you reduce the chance you might knock your drink glasses over. Bad table manners kill more interviews because they are so tricky to manage. Get a copy of Emily Post and read up on table manners if you think you may get inflicted with the dreaded meal interview.

10. Last but not least: While it is generally said that you should not say no while in an interview, if you find yourself interviewing someplace where you feel very uncomfortable and you know you won't accept the offer even if you were living on lentils and peanut butter, it's better to let the interviewer know as soon as you do.

That being said, don't cut yourself off without first being very clear that this is what you want to do, because once you do say no, the opportunity is gone.

Things to Remember: Best Practices

This is the section of the book where we remind you to dress warmly, always keep your feet dry, and never take candy from strangers driving vans.

No, seriously, if you are planning to enter, thinking about entering, or have already entered the great world of fashion, there are some things you should learn, remember, and hold close to you at all times.

Just like all of the things your mother told you about staying warm and eating right, learning the best practices about your portfolio design and development will save you a lot of hassle and a lot of grief.

So, from the top:

1. Always keep your original artwork someplace safe. Whether that is at the top of Mt. Kilimanjaro or just in a locked drawer in your home filing cabinet, know where your artwork is, and keep it safe.

2. Don't leave your portfolio lying around unattended when you have it out in public. It's expensive. In design school, it could get stolen; elsewhere, you may just forget you have it and leave it.

However it vanishes, it will be gone, and if it 'just vanishes' before you have an interview, it's going to be very difficult for you to show your work to your interviewer.

3. Pick one orientation for your portfolio—either portrait (vertical) or landscape (horizontal)—and stick with it religiously. Best practices say you can allow the viewer to flip the book once, but we don't even like that idea when, with a little forward thinking, you can just make sure everything is either portrait or landscape.

4. Put some thought and money into your portfolio binding. It matters. A lot.

5. Use more than one portfolio if you have more than one area of expertise. Great with mask making? Cool, but that work doesn't belong in your fashion portfolio. Showcase your work accordingly.

6. Plan ahead—your portfolio will take time and money to put together. Don't get to the end of your degree without a portfolio. Things get harder if you graduate with no job and no portfolio.

7. Carefully think through how you want your portfolio to 'read'. Then begin developing collections and stories that fit that vision. Be careful about what you add—not all stories need to go into your portfolio.

8. Don't get discouraged. Putting together a good portfolio is hard. It may take you a year to get a good portfolio together—start early and keep working on it. Yes, it's hard. We know.

Start early anyway. You can always go par-tay with friends once you have a job. On the other hand, if you don't have a job, that par-tay is going to be kind of depressing what with no money to pay for clothing of appropriate fabulosity, cover charge or drinkies.

9. Budget wisely. Yes, that hot pink maribou boa is the essence of fabulosity and of course you just need it, but do you need it more than you need a finished portfolio? Probably not, and without the portfolio it will be difficult to obtain a paying job that lets you buy all the other fabulosities out there.

Budget and plan for your portfolio, get it done, and get a job. Then you can have all the fabulous maribou boas your heart desires and your pocket book can manage.

10. Ask for help: your teachers should be thrilled to give you feedback about your portfolio. After all, your employment in the industry reflects well on their teaching.

11. Don't ask for help: your classmates. While undoubtedly wonderful people who want nothing but the best for you, they are competitors in the job market, and are at least as confused as you are about this portfolio thing. Actually more confused, because you bought and hopefully read this book and didn't just look at the pretty pictures.

Asking for feedback, input or help from your classmates can be a dangerous thing. Even if they are supa-genius, it's not to say they want to be supa-genius for you. Keep in mind, during your portfolio class, your classmates will be reviewing your work and offering their commentary on specific drawings and projects.

You will likely be required to present your student portfolio to your classmates repeatedly throughout your final semester, but this is a very different situation from asking a classmate to help you with your professional portfolio.

12. And last, but not least: Think creatively: there are a lot of great new technology resources available now, with many more emerging. Maybe you will be best able to present your design concepts using a mobile application sent from your mobile device!

Put your portfolio on a netbook—you can make a PowerPoint® presentation or a video showcasing your work, which will let you quickly and easily change your book.

PonyTale

Spring 2010

Pony Tale is a girls' headwear line. The full product line is not shown here, rather, the mood board, the color story, and the print development are shown.

The girls' marketplace is substantial, and there are certain colors that need to appear in this branch of children's wear. For example, pinks and lavenders are a must, followed by aqua and/or blues. I added a green, because I wanted to stay with the 'rainbow' effect of the Pony Tale mood board. The type of the collection reflects what the viewer should expect to see: a collection which is feminine, juvenile, and fun.

And of course, the prints reflect the season and the gender class: fluffy clouds are spring-like, and polkadots are an evergreen favorite. Note the print callouts, and the layout of the prints in their colorways. Had the remainder of the product line been included, there would be a trim, a material, and the style boards as well as just the print boards.

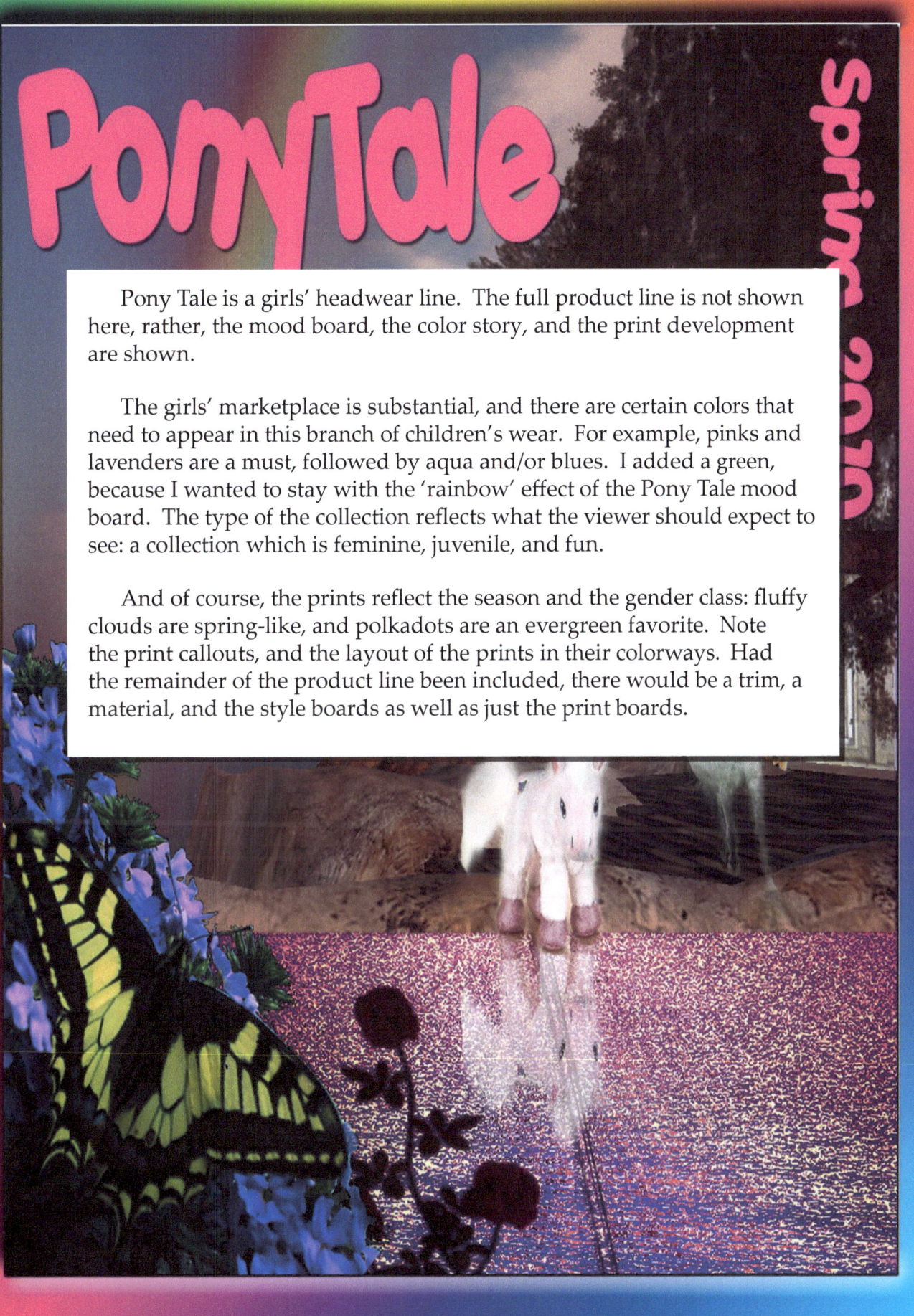

PonyTale

Spring 2010

PonyTale

Spring 2010

Bright	PMS 226 C
Pansy	PMS 512 C
Bluebird	PMS 654 C
Grass	PMS 364 C
Daffodil	PMS 604 C
Tulip	PMS 223 C
Lilac	PMS 514 C
Sky	PMS 649 C
Clover	PMS 359 C
Sunlight	PMS 600 C
Soot	PMS Black
Arctic White	PMS White

PonyTale

Spring 2010

PRINTS

Polka Dots

- Daffodil
- Grass
- Bluebird
- Pansy
- Bright

Clouds

- Sunlight
- Clover
- Sky
- Lilac
- Tulip

PonyTale

Spring 2010

Print Layouts

Polka Dot Screenprint

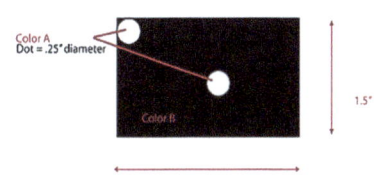

Color A — Dot = .25" diameter
Color B
1.5"
2.25"

☐ Color A   ■ Color B

Clouds Screenprint

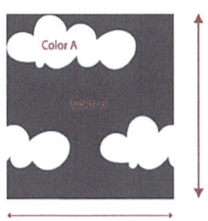

Color A
2"
2"

☐ Color A   ■ Color B

Chapter Six
Beyond the Book

Chapter Six: Beyond the Book

Resources

We mentioned earlier that there are many new tools and resources available to you to help you present your portfolio. The following two sections will help you find new ways of presenting your work, and in some cases may even define your career!

American Apparel and Footwear Association
www.apparelandfootwear.org/
1601 North Kent Street, Suite 1200
Arlington VA 22209

The AAFA is the national trade association representing apparel, footwear, sewn products companies, and their suppliers. It promotes and seeks to enhance members companies' competitiveness, productivity and profitability in the global marketplace. They have any number of useful links on their web site, particularly about statistics and restricted substances.

Apparel Search
apparelsearch.com

Apparel Search is an extensive aggregator of links for a range of topics within the industry. You can find everything here from trend services to factories, and everything in between.

Color Association of the United States
315 W 39th Street, Studio 506
New York, NY, 10018
(212) 947-7774
www.colorassociation.com

The Color Association of the United States is a membership organization quartered in New York city which creates and delivers global color intelligence across 73 industries, not just fashion. This organization is a forecast agent and provides specialized education to help insure that its members make successful color decisions for brand identity, product, communications, and spatial environments.

Dover Publications
31 East 2nd Street
Mineola, NY 11501
www.doverpublications.com

Dover is an amazing resource. Offering more than 40 years of publications, their catalog includes not only wonderful fashion books and resources, but an increasing number of terribly useful book/CD combinations. Some of their most recent explorations include Clip Art, Photoshop brushes and CDs of vector-based prints, images and patterns.

Materia
Binnenhof 62D
1412 LC Naarden
The Netherlands
T +31 (0)35 71 21 732
F +31 (0)35 69 22 678
info@materia.nl
www.materia.nl

Materia is an amazing resource of new and innovative materials for the design industries. Materia includes the Inspiration Centre, where materials can be experience in real life, and an extensive database that is free to use. Materia also publishes newsletters, publications and presents on topics of innovative materials.

Fierce is a collection of virtual goods developed for sale in game platforms. I included it here because the development of the collection followed the same lines as developing an accessories collection, and because all designers should be looking at designing not only for the physical marketplace, but also for the burgeoning virtual goods marketplace.

Fierce is a better swimwear collection designed for women aged 18-30. It incorporates plain, dyed, and thermo-foiled 4-way stretch knit as the primary material. The mood board reflects a fiercely sexy woman, and the swimwear included also reflects a woman who isn't afraid to show her body. Bright, vibrant color choices along with an evergreen cheetah print developed in multiple colorways make Fierce a force on the (virtual) runway. You can see the Fierce models strutting their stuff at the Black Dress Technology website, www.blackdresstechnology.com.

Note how the font chosen for the fierce collection reflects an edgy, trendy feel. The colors chosen for the mood board along with the iconography reflect what the viewer expects to see in the collection. The use of a girl in a bathing suit also sets expectations of what the viewer should see in the collection.

Fierce was never developed for a physical production run, but rather to showcase Black Dress Technology's Virtual Runway™ product. The collection is available as virtual goods for use in the OpenSim and Second Life immersive 3D platforms.

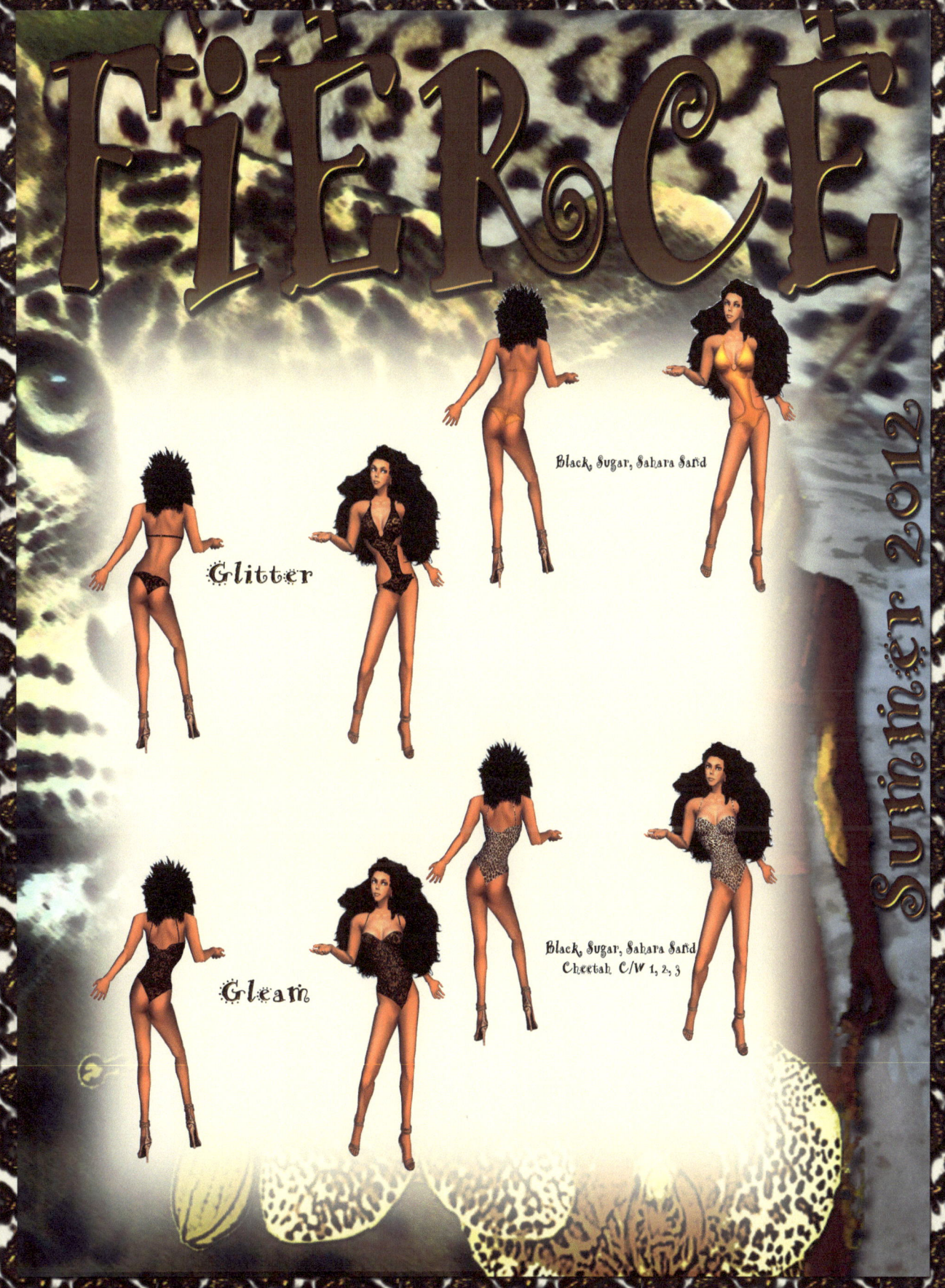

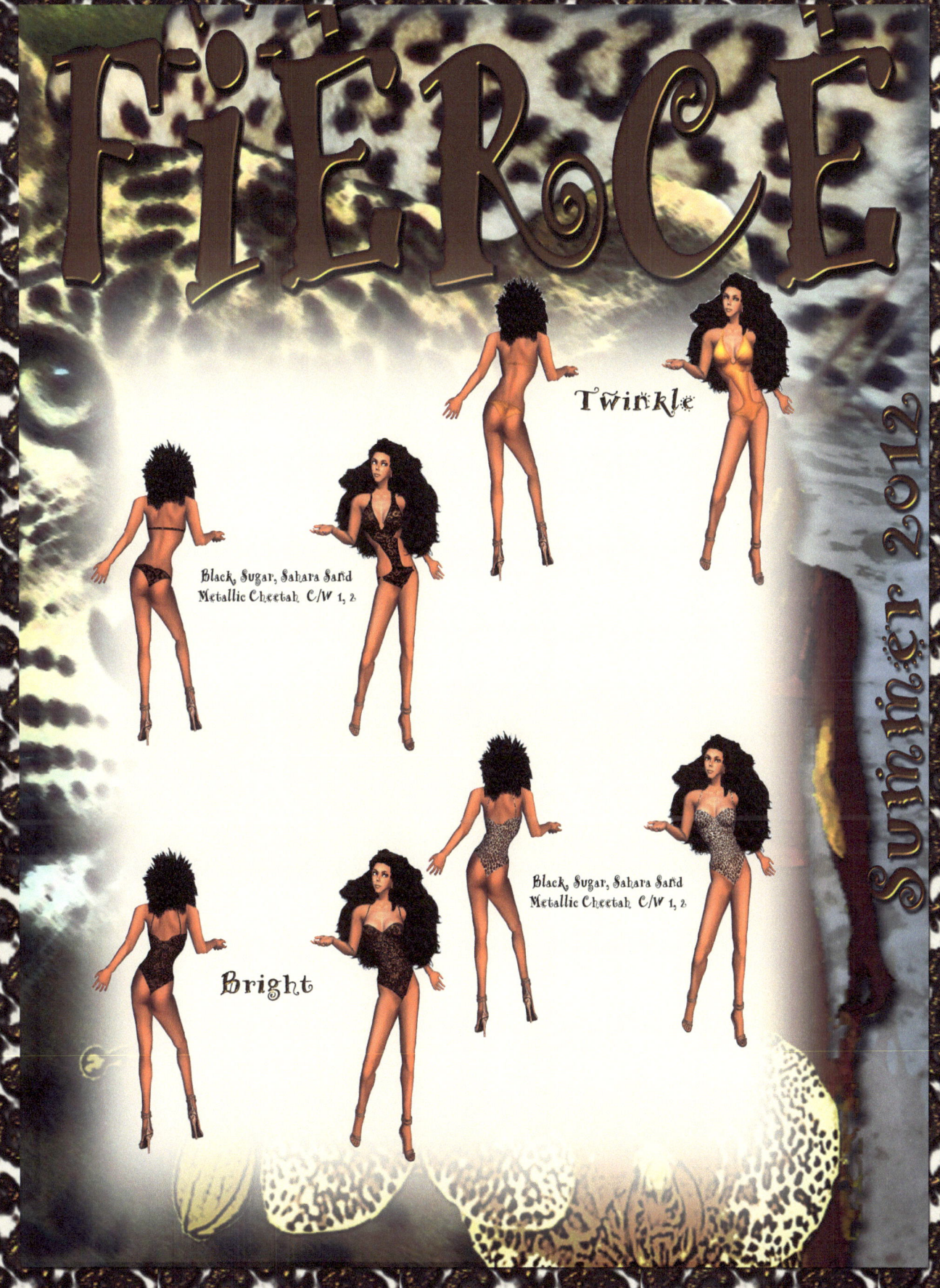

Morgue File

www.morguefile.com

Morgue File offers designers free images for use in their creative work, for inspiration, and for reference. All images on the MorgueFile.com web site are royalty (but not copyright) free and may be used for noncommercial work (like your portfolio). Check their license if you need to use any images for commercial work (i.e., if someone is paying you). High resolution and great quality, Morgue File is an awesome resource.

Mudpie

www.mudpie.co.uk/

Mudpie is one of the premier trend services in the apparel industry, focusing on delivering timely, topical trends for the adult, youth and children marketplaces. In addition to offering trend direction, they also offer superb trend books which include graphic, print, pattern, and color forecasting.

Promostyl
www.promostyl.com

Promostyle is a French trend research and design agency. Promostyle tends to offer a uniquely Parisian look at the apparel industry, and is a wonderful resource for designers with a European focus.

Style.com
www.style.com

With ten years of fashion and style in their database, every designer out there needs to know about style.com. Search through their extensive archives for the perfect runway show images or explore the trends and shopping forecasts. You can search on designers, models or even celebrities to see what your favorite 'it' people are doing and wearing.

Trendhunter

www.trendhunter.com

Trendhunter differs from most of the trend organizations by being virally lead and evolved by its active community of 40,000 trend hunters. The Trend hunter web site offers inspiration and reference for aspiring and established designers alike, as we look for the next 'it' thing.

WGSN

Greater London House
Hampstead Road
London
NW1 7EJ
Tel:+44 (0)20 7728 5822
www.wgsn.com

WGSN is a leading online trend-analysis and research service providing creative and business intelligence for the apparel, style, design and retail industries. With more than 12 years of experience, it offers a database with more than 5,000,000 images and more than 650,000 pages of information.

Women's Wear Daily

www.wwd.com

Women's Wear Daily is the premiere publication of the American apparel industry. Published in hard copy every day, online subscriptions are also available. If you subscribe to no other publication, make it WWD.

Tools

Adobe Systems Incorporated
345 Park Avenue
San Jose, CA 95110-2704
Tel: 408-536-6000
Fax: 408-537-6000
www.adobe.com

Adobe makes the industry standard suite of software that enables users to design and develop amazing work, collaborate effectively, and deliver virtually anywhere. The Creative Suite 5 series includes both Photoshop, and Illustrator, and depending on the exact version, may include Dream Weaver or InDesign as well as other Adobe products.

Audacity
www.audacityteam.org

Audacity® is free, open source software for recording and editing sounds. It is available for Mac OS X, Microsoft Windows, GNU/Linux, and other operating systems. It is perfect to use when you want to create voice over for your videos.

Autodesk

Autodesk, Inc.
111 McInnis Parkway
San Rafael, CA 94903
www.autodesk.com

Autodesk develops two important 3D modeling tools, Maya and 3DS Max. Both offer a comprehensive suite of 3D modeling, simulation, and other effects.

Avid/Pinnacle's Studio 12

280 North Bernardo Avenue
Mountain View, California 94043
Tel: 650-526-1600
Fax: 650-526-1601

Now even simpler to use, the user-friendly drag-and-drop interface in Pinnacle Studio makes it easy to create high-quality videos with music, stunning new montage themes, transitions, animations and effects. The Studio products are powered by the same technology used in Avid®, the entertainment industry's leading application.

Black Dress Design Studio ™
www.blackdresstechnology.com

Black Dress Technology offers Black Dress Design Studio ™, a simple and easy 3D modeling application that allows designers to quickly prototype their designs in a fully immersive 3D environment. Couple that with concurrent technical specification development, delivered through web page or PDF, and Black Dress Design Studio makes a designer's life easier and her design go faster.

Blender
Entrepotdok 57A
1018 AD Amsterdam
the Netherlands
www.blender.org

Blender is an open source (free) 3-D modeling creative suite that runs on all major operating systems. Blender is a powerful piece of free software which produces many of the same results that Autodesk's Maya and 3DS Max do.

CreateSpace
1200 12th Ave South
Suite 1200
Seattle, WA 98144
www.createspace.com

CreateSpace provides free tools to help you self-publish and distribute your books, DVDs, CDs, video downloads and MP3s on-demand on Amazon.com and other web sites. You can also use it to just print your own work for your own purpose. Create Space is a good service but not quite as flexible as MagCloud. If you aren't planning to print your publication as an actual ISBN-requiring publication, you are better off using MagCloud.

Fraps
www.fraps.com

Fraps offers one of the best on-line video capture tools out there. It has an ad-based free version or an inexpensive commercial version which you can use to quickly and easily make video of your work. It only works on Windows, so Mac users are out of luck.

MagCloud

Hewlett-Packard Company
3000 Hanover Street, MS 1051
Palo Alto, CA 94304
Tel: (650) 857-1501
Fax: (650) 236-9855
www.magcloud.com

MagCloud is an awesome service from HP that enables novice or experienced creators to publish their work on-demand with no upfront set up fees or costs, no minimum print runs and no ISBN required. MagCloud is perfect to print your portfolio on high quality stock with high quality, calibrated inks.

Makerbot

www.makerbot.com

MakerBot Industries offers up the ultimate Do-It-yourself open source 3D printer. The Makerbot can product items up to 4"x4"x6", and it prints with easily obtainable ABS plastic. The Makerbots are sold as kits, so if you aren't mechanically inclined or don't have a friend who can help with assembly, you may want to skip the Makerbot. If however, you appreciate a challenge, the MakerBot will give you a desktop (almost) 3D printer you can use to create your own trims and hardware prototypes, right from the comfort of your own home.

OpenSim
www.opensimulator.org

OpenSimulator is an open source multi-platform, multi-user 3D application server. It can be used to create a virtual environment (or world) which can be accessed through a variety of clients, on multiple protocols. OpenSimulator allows virtual world developers to customize their worlds using the technologies they feel work best.

Shapeways
www.shapeways.com

Shapeways offers on-line services to turn your 3D digital files into 3D reality. Upload your design, and Shapeways will print and ship it to you within 10 working days. Shapeways is not inexpensive, but if you want to showcase some trim or hardware ideas in your portfolio, you can use a range of materials from plastic to glass.

Spoonflower, Inc.
2810 Meridian Parkway, suite 130
Durham, NC 27713, USA
+1 (919) 321-2949
www.spoonflower.com

Spoonflower is a domestic short-run digital printer of fabrics. Using their own palette of colors, Spoonflower uses eco-friendly, water-based pigment inks to print your textile designs on your choice of their fabrics. Lead times can take up to 3 weeks when they are very busy, so plan ahead. They offer great service and you can have anything from a swatch size to a dress length printed using your digital files. You don't even have to do separations, and because there are no screens to create, you can use as many colors as you want!

Vimeo
c/o IAC Consumer Applications & Portals, Inc.
One North Lexington, 9th Floor
White Plains, NY, 10601
www.vimeo.com

Vimeo provides a community-based web site and tool for creators to share their videos with an easy to use tool.

Virtual Runway ™
www.blackdresstechnology.com

Virtual Runway allows designers to quickly create digital runway shows or fashion showrooms where they can show their designs to everyone in their development pipeline, making the development process go more smoothly and quickly. VR can also be used as a marketing channel, enabling designers to invite their consumers in for market focus groups or to presell a collection before it is ever physically sampled. Couple that with the ability to create short videos for Youtube or blog, and Virtual Runway allows designers' creative vision to take flight!

Youtube
901 Cherry Ave.
San Bruno, CA 94066
USA
Phone: +1 650-253-0000
www.youtube.com

Youtube® is the world's most popular online video sharing tool. It acts as a distribution platform for original content creators of all sorts.

Conclusion

By now you should have a good idea of how you want to develop your portfolio for your professional career. A portfolio is a living document which is never done.

As your skills become stronger and as you develop more work, you will change out previous visual stories and insert others. You will add and remove media coverage as you receive it. And you should keep your portfolio up-to-date, because even when you are happy at a current position, you should always be prepared for new opportunities, however they may find you.

There is nothing is worse than scrambling to try to get your portfolio changed for an interview, so make it a habit to tweak your portfolio on a monthly basis.

Also, don't be afraid to try new products or services which may help you showcase your talent. As a fashion designer, you are expected to lead new trends, so don't be afraid to be out there with new ways to present and sell yourself and your skills.

Last, but not least, start early to develop your portfolio. Waiting to the last month or even last quarter of your final semester will not let you create a portfolio that really lets you sell yourself.

The whole point of design school is to let you work in the industry, and for most designers, that means developing a portfolio that allows themselves to showcase their ability. Even if you do not wish to work for others, the skills required to develop a portfolio will be useful in other ways, such as developing the required marketing pieces for your own collections.

Whatever your desired career path is, best of luck to you as you pursue your dreams!

Author Shenlei E. Winkler

Twitter:

Shenlei

Blog:

http://www.shenlei.com

Linked in:

http://www.linkedin.com/pub/shenlei-winkler/0/253/6b7

Consulting for portfolio review
for admission to college available
on case-by-case basis.

www.ingramcontent.com/pod-product-compliance
Lightning Source LLC
Chambersburg PA
CBHW040902020526
44114CB00037B/31